LIST OF LOW SODIUM FOODS

ULTIMATE GUIDE TO NO & LOW SODIUM FOODS FOR ADULTS & SENIORS, LOW SALT RENAL DIET & DASH DIET COMPANION

JULIA MEADOWS

ABOUT THE AUTHOR

Julia Meadows is a senior life coach and Wellness expert at the WellnessMastership.com, a life coaching business based in London, England.

Wellness Mastership teaches clients on consciousness, lifting your vibration, the real law of attraction (updated), and the art of living a better life. Through our teaching we have helped clients worldwide gain a better advantage, and help develop themselves and achieve more from want they desire.

We're in the changing lives business.

SODIUM TRACKER

www.amazon.com/stores/Julie-Meadows/author/B08DQ8NK7L

DATE		M T W T F S S		WATER INTAKE

WEIGHT		SLEEP	

	FOOD & DRINKS	SERVING SIZE	SODIUM	CALORIES	PROTEIN	CARBS
BREAKFAST						
	BREAKFAST TOTAL					
SNACK						
	SNACK TOTAL					
LUNCH						
SNACK						
	SNACK TOTAL					
DINNER						
	DINNER TOTAL					
	DAILY TOTAL					

Free Bonus from Julie Meadows <juliameadowsauthor@gmail.com>

BLOOD PRESSURE		
TIME	SYS/DIA	PULSE

NOTES

KEEP TRACK OF YOUR SALT INTAKE!

SCAN ME FOR A BONUS

https://bonus.mindsetmastership.com/low-sodium-food

We are excited to offer a free sodium tracker bonus to help you reach your health goals. Our sodium tracker bonus is an easy-to-use tool that allows you to track your daily sodium intake and make informed choices about the foods you eat. With this bonus, you can identify high-sodium foods, track your progress, and make healthier choices for a healthier you.

CLAIM YOUR FREE BONUS HERE NOW!

https://bonus.mindsetmastership.com/low-sodium-food

WANT A COPY OF MY NEW EBOOK?

Email me:
juliameadowsauthor@gmail.com

"Wherever you go, go with all your heart."
— **Confucius**

MASTERSHIP BOOKS

UK | USA | Canada | Ireland | Australia
India | New Zealand | South Africa | China

Mastership Books is part of the United Arts Publishing House group of
companies based in London, England, UK.
First published by Mastership Books (London, UK), 2023
Text Copyright © United Arts Publishing

Cover design by Rich © United Arts Publishing (UK)
Text and internal design by Rich © United Arts Publishing (UK)

Image credits reserved.
Colour separation by Spitting Image Design Studio

Printed and bound in Great Britain
National Publications Association of Britain
London, England, United Kingdom.

Paper design UAP
A723.5

Title: Low Sodium Food

Design, Bound & Printed:
London, England,
Great Britain.

Low Sodium, GI, and LDL Foods

GET A FREE AUDIOBOOK

EMAIL SUBJECT LINE:

"LOW SODIUM FOOD"

TO

juliameadowsauthor@gmail.com

CONTENTS

INTRODUCTION

Welcome to the world of low-sodium eating! Whether you have been prescribed a low-sodium diet by your doctor or want to reduce your salt intake for a healthier lifestyle, you've come to the right place. Sodium is an essential nutrient that is crucial in regulating fluid balance and blood pressure. However, most people consume more sodium than their bodies need, leading to high blood pressure and other health problems.

This book will show you how to consume less sodium while you enjoy delicious, flavorful food. We'll start with an overview of electrolytes and their effects on our health so you can fully understand the importance of a low-sodium diet. You'll learn how to read food labels, identify high-sodium foods, and the best ways to use substitutions so you can still enjoy your favorite meals. We'll also explore the powerful effects of this diet on blood pressure and other related chronic diseases, while providing you with tips and strategies for reducing your sodium intake.

We've also included various delicious low-sodium recipes to help you make healthy eating easy and enjoyable. There are recipes for breakfast, lunch, dinner, and even snacks so you can prepare them daily for yourself or your family. Along the way, you'll get tips, tricks, and recipes to stay within our healthy eating plate guideline. You'll have all the information you need to make small, daily dietary changes that should lead to significant, long-term results.

So, if you're ready to embark on a low-sodium journey, grab a fork. Reducing sodium intake can be simple and even delicious with the right tools and information.

Ready to learn about low-sodium eating? Let's get started!

Dear Reader,

As independent authors, it's often difficult to gather reviews compared with much bigger publishers.

Therefore, please leave a review on the platform where you bought this book.

KINDLE:

<u>LEAVE A REVIEW HERE < click here ></u>

Many thanks,

Author Team

1

OVERVIEW OF ELECTROLYTES

The weight of the body is mainly made up of water. Medical professionals say the body's water is contained in several fluid compartments. There are three major compartments:

- Fluid within cells
- The fluid around cells
- Blood

The body must prevent excessive variations in fluid levels in certain regions to operate correctly. Some minerals are essential as electrolytes, particularly macrominerals (minerals the body requires in relatively high quantities). Minerals are called electrolytes, to carry an electric charge when dissolved in fluids like blood. The sodium, potassium, chloride, and bicarbonate found in blood electrolytes assist in regulating neuron and muscle activity and maintaining water and acid-base balance.

. . .

Because the quantity of fluid a compartment holds relies on the amount (concentration) of electrolytes in it, electrolytes, especially sodium, aid the body in maintaining appropriate fluid levels in the fluid compartments.

Fluid enters that compartment if the electrolyte content is high (a process called osmosis). Likewise, fluid goes out of that compartment if the electrolyte concentration is low. The body may actively transfer electrolytes into or out of cells to modify fluid levels.

Therefore, maintaining a fluid balance between the compartments requires having electrolytes in the proper concentrations (electrolyte balance). The kidneys aid in maintaining electrolyte concentrations by filtering electrolytes and water from the blood, restoring some to circulation, and excreting any excess in the urine.

As a result, the kidneys aid in balancing the body's regular intake and excretion of electrolytes and water. Disorders may arise if the electrolyte balance is off. For instance, the following may cause an electrolyte imbalance:

- Excessive or inadequate hydration
- Utilizing certain medications
- Having certain liver, kidney, or cardiac conditions
- Receiving excessive quantities of intravenous fluids or feedings

Electrolytes

In water, compounds known as "electrolytes" take on a net positive or negative electrical charge, respectively. Multiple cellular and non-cellular fluid balances and chemical reactions rely on them to operate normally. They're also an essential part of making a diagnosis for a variety of illnesses and ailments.

Electrolytes: What are they?

Electrolytes naturally have a positive or negative electrical charge that changes when water dissolves. Because water makes up around 60% of the average adult's body, electrolytes may be found in almost every bodily fluid and cell. Multiple cellular and non-cellular fluid balances and chemical reactions rely on them to operate normally. Electrolytes, or their components, are ingested by food and drink. Your kidneys remove extra electrolytes from your body and filter them into your urine. When you sweat, you also lose electrolytes.

How do electrolytes function?

Your muscles contract because your cells employ electrolytes to carry electrical charges. Chemical processes are also aided by the exact electrical charges, particularly regarding hydration and the equilibrium of fluids within and outside of cells. The fundamental idea behind electrolytes is that specific chemical components may naturally contain a positive or negative electrical charge. When a liquid has specific components dissolved in it, the liquid becomes electrically conductible.

Saltwater, which readily conducts electricity, is one illustration of this. The positive and negative charges of sodium and chlorine, which make up salt, cancel each other out when mixed. Ions are atoms having an electrical charge (positive ions are called cations, while negative ions are called anions). The sodium and chlorine atoms divide when salt is dissolved in water, reverting to their original positive and negative charges. Because the sodium and chlorine ions have opposing electrical charges, electricity jumps between them rather than between the water molecules. Electrolytes assist in maintaining equilibrium in your body at the most fundamental chemical level. Your body employs ions to move chemical substances into and out of cells as electricity moves from one place to another in salt water.

What are the main elements of the electrolyte?

Your body requires several essential components to maintain appropriate electrolyte levels. The primary components are listed in the following section, each denoted as positive (+) or negative (-), along with the effects of too much or too little of it.

Sodium (+)

Your cells' ability to maintain the proper fluid balance is greatly aided by sodium. Additionally, it aids food absorption by cells, and it is the electrolyte ion that is most prevalent in the body.

- Hypernatremia (excessive sodium intake): Can result in unconsciousness, convulsions, extreme reflexes, and changes in behavior.
- Hyponatremia (inadequate sodium): confusion, irritability, decreased reflexes, nausea and vomiting, seizures, and coma.

Magnesium (+)

Your cells benefit from magnesium when they convert nutrients into energy. Magnesium is essential for the functioning of your muscles and brain.

- Hypermagnesemia (too much magnesium): cardiac arrest, impaired reflexes, arrhythmias, and alterations in heart rhythm (your heart stops).
- Hypomagnesemia (insufficient magnesium): Weak muscles, twitching, loss of control, and irregular heartbeats. This often occurs when there are calcium and potassium deficits.

Potassium (+)

Along with sodium, potassium is used by your cells, and a potassium ion departs from a cell when a sodium ion arrives, and vice versa. Additionally, potassium plays a crucial role in how well your heart works, and severe cardiac issues might result from too much or too little.

- Hyperkalemia (excess potassium): Muscle weakness, disorientation, irregular heartbeats, and weakness (arrhythmias).
- Hypokalemia (insufficient potassium): Symptoms include muscle weakness and cramps, unusual thirst and frequent urination, disorientation, and fainting when rising too rapidly. At larger concentrations, cardiac arrhythmias become a significant risk, and muscle tissue breaks down (a disease known as

rhabdomyolysis, which may seriously harm your kidneys).

Calcium (+)

Although it is an essential component of your body, calcium does more than only support healthy bones and teeth. It's also utilized to regulate your heartbeat, send instructions to your nerves, control your muscles, and more. Numerous symptoms affecting various bodily systems might result from too much or too little calcium in the blood.

Hypercalcemia (too much calcium)

- Brain: Headache, weariness, apathy, and bewilderment.
- Digestive tract: vomiting, nausea, and constipation.
- Kidneys: a propensity for frequent urination, kidney stones, and kidney failure.
- Heart: a variety of arrhythmias, some of which may be serious.
- Skeletal: Aches and pains in the joints and bones.

Hypocalcemia (not enough calcium)

- Brain: Disorientation and altered behavior.
- Muscles: abnormally quick reflexes, lack of control over muscles, twitching, and spasms in

the throat muscles that make it difficult to breathe or talk.

Chloride (-)

The second-most prevalent ion in the body is chloride, the term for the chlorine ion. The fluid balance between the inside and outside of your cells also depends on it, and it contributes to preserving the body's natural pH equilibrium.

Hyperchloremia (too much chloride)

Acidosis, or excessively acidic blood, may result from this. It causes disorientation, faster, deeper breathing, nausea, vomiting, and exhaustion. Usually, too much or too little potassium is the cause of this.

- When hyperkalemia is involved: Too much potassium may result in severe renal damage or even kidney failure.
- When linked to hypokalemia: Low potassium levels may result in diarrhea, pancreatic fluid leakage, and other severe urinary tract issues.

Hypochloremia (not enough chloride)

- Alkalosis, a condition where your blood becomes more acidic, is brought on by this. Typically, vomiting or hyponatremia causes it. Apathy, disorientation, arrhythmias, and twitching or lack of control of the muscles are signs of alkalosis.

Phosphate (-)

Phosphate, a molecule made of phosphorus, is essential for moving molecules and chemical substances outside your cells. It's a vital part of the nucleotide molecules that serve as the building blocks of your DNA and helps your cells metabolize the food you eat.

- Hyperphosphatemia (excess phosphate): When this occurs, your body attempts to utilize calcium as a replacement for phosphorus, which often results in hypocalcemia. It usually doesn't manifest until it is severe, and symptoms of hypocalcemia frequently accompany this. It may also be connected to persistent itching.
- Hypophosphatemia (low phosphate): Muscle weakness is often this condition's first sign. The symptoms get more severe as it worsens. Seizures, diminished heart function, breathing difficulties, and rhabdomyolysis (the breakdown of muscle tissue, which may severely harm the kidneys) are a few of them (caused by muscle weakness).

Bicarbonate (-)

Not all of the carbon dioxides your body produces are transported to your lungs so that you may exhale them. As an alternative, part of it is recycled into bicarbonate, which your body requires to maintain a proper pH level in your blood.

- Acidosis. When your blood is overly acidic, acidosis results from a lack of bicarbonate. You will also breathe more quickly and deeply due to exhaustion, nausea, and vomiting. Confusion may also result from it.
- Alkalosis. When you have an alkalosis due to excess bicarbonate, your blood becomes too basic. Confusion, apathy, arrhythmias, and jerking of the muscles are symptoms.

Overview of the Function of Sodium in the Body

One of the electrolytes or minerals the body requires in relatively high concentrations is sodium. When electrolytes are dissolved in bodily fluids like blood, they acquire an electric charge. (See also Electrolytes Overview.) The blood and the surrounding fluid cells contain the majority of the sodium in the body, and sodium aids the body's regular fluid equilibrium (see About Body Water). Sodium is essential for healthy neuron and muscle function.

The main ways that the body loses salt are via sweat and urine and through meals and liquids. Healthy kidneys keep the body's sodium level constant by regulating the quantity of sodium expelled in the urine. The overall amount of sodium in the body is impacted when sodium intake and loss are out of balance. Sodium levels (concentration) in the blood may:

- Too little (hyponatremia)
- Too much (hypernatremia)

Controlling blood volume

Blood volume and the quantity of fluid around cells are influenced by the body's overall amount of sodium. The body constantly monitors the blood's volume and salt content. Sensors in the heart, blood arteries, and kidneys may detect increases in either when they reach unhealthy levels. These sensors then prompt the kidneys to enhance salt excretion, lowering blood volume to normal. The sensors activate systems to boost blood volume when sodium concentration or blood volume falls too low. The following is a list of these mechanisms:

- The kidneys encourage the release of the hormone aldosterone from the adrenal glands. The kidneys retain sodium and eliminate potassium when aldosterone is present. When salt is retained, less urine is made, which increases blood volume.
- Vasopressin is produced by the pituitary gland (sometimes called antidiuretic hormone). The kidneys save water due to vasopressin.

Keeping the balance of fluids and sodium in older people

The body's capacity to maintain an appropriate level of sodium and fluid decreases with age for several reasons:

- Reduced thirst: As individuals age, they experience thirst less rapidly or strongly, possibly leading to dehydration.
- Kidney changes: As kidneys age, they may lose their ability to concentrate urine and recover water and electrolytes. As a consequence, more water may be expelled in urine.
- Less fluid in the body: Older adults have less fluid. In elderly persons, just 45% of body weight is fluid, compared to 60% in younger ones. As a result of this alteration, an older person may have more severe effects from a little loss of fluid and salt, such as that which might happen from a fever or from not eating enough or drinking enough (sometimes for just a day or two).
- Inability to access water: Some elderly persons have physical issues that make it difficult to quench their thirst. Others can have dementia, making it difficult to acknowledge or express their thirst. These folks could be forced to rely on others to provide water.
- Medicines: Many elderly individuals use medications to treat high blood pressure, diabetes mellitus, or cardiac conditions. These medications might cause the body to expel extra fluid or can amplify the negative consequences of fluid loss.

The scenarios above may lead to fluid loss or inadequate fluid intake, resulting in a high blood salt level (hypernatremia) and dehydration. Hypernatremia is more prevalent in elderly adults since these circumstances are more typical. In elderly persons, hypernatremia is poorly tolerated and, in extreme cases, may cause disorientation, coma, and even death.Renal disease, liver issues, and excess fluid retention (fluid overload) are all conditions that are more common in older adults. Consequently, excess fluid and salt are also more common in older persons.

Older persons are more likely to have hyponatremia or low blood salt levels. Hyponatremia often develops when the body retains too much fluid, like heart failure or liver illness. Taking some diuretics, such as thiazide diuretics like hydrochlorothiazide, may also cause hyponatremia in elderly persons, especially if the kidneys are not working properly. Diuretics, sometimes known as water pills, aid in the body's removal of extra fluid. Inpatient low-sodium intravenous fluids or liquid nutritional supplements may also result in hyponatremia in elderly patients.

Sodium and Salt

About 40% sodium and 60% chloride make up salt, often known as sodium chloride. It adds taste to meals and serves as a stabilizer and binder. Salt is a food preservative because germs cannot thrive in its presence. The human body needs a small quantity of sodium to convey nerve impulses, contract and relax muscles, and maintain the right ratio of water and minerals. We need 500 mg of salt daily for these essential processes. However, too much salt may cause high blood pressure, heart disease, and stroke.

· · ·

Additionally, it may result in calcium losses, some of which may come from the bone. Approximately 3400 mg of sodium, or at least 1.5 teaspoons of salt, is consumed daily by most Americans, significantly more than our need.

Recommended Amounts

According to the US Dietary Reference Intakes, insufficient information exists to determine a salt RDA or hazardous level (aside from chronic disease risk). As a result, a Tolerable Upper Intake Level (UL), the daily intake most likely to be safe for health, has not been defined. Guidelines for Appropriate Intakes (AI) of sodium were developed using the lowest sodium intake levels utilized in randomized controlled studies that did not demonstrate a deficit but also permitted an adequate intake of wholesome foods naturally containing sodium. The AI is 1,500 mg daily for males, women, and pregnant women at least 14 years old. Based on the findings that a lower salt intake lowers the risk of cardiovascular disease and high blood pressure, a Chronic Disease Risk Reduction (CDRR) Intake has also been devised. In the general healthy population, lowering salt consumption below the CDRR is anticipated to reduce the risk of chronic illness. The highest daily intake recommended by the CDRR for reducing the risk of chronic diseases in adults 14 years of age and older and pregnant women is 2,300 milligrams.

Types of Salt

Due to their density, finely crushed salts often contain more sodium than coarser salts. Check the Nutrition Facts label for the most accurate amount since salt levels vary significantly across brands.

Approximate amount of sodium in 1 teaspoon
Iodized table salt, fine
It has 2,300 mg of sodium

Kosher salt, course
It has 1,920 mg of sodium

Kosher salt, fine, Diamond Crystal®†
It has 1,120 mg of sodium

Sea salt, fine
It has 2,120 mg of sodium

Sea salt, course
It has 1,560 mg of sodium

Pink (Himalayan) salt
It has 2,200 mg of sodium

Black salt
It has 1,150-2,200 mg of sodium

. . .

Fleur de sel
   It has 1,560-2,320 mg of sodium

Potassium salt (salt substitute)
   It has 0 mg (contains 2,760-3,180 mg potassium) of sodium

† Brand names on this list are included for reference; they are not a recommendation. The Nutrition Source doesn't advocate for any particular brands.

Food Sources

Generally speaking, sodium is a nutrient you don't need to seek actively. Salt isn't often found in foods that are eaten whole, such as fruit, vegetables, whole grains, nuts, meat, and dairy products. Most of our meals come from professionally prepared foods, not salt added during home cooking or mealtimes. The following are the top 10 foods with salt, as suggested by CDC (Centers for Disease Control and Prevention): savory snacks (chips, popcorn, pretzels, crackers), pizza, sandwiches, soups, burritos, tacos, bread and rolls, chicken, cheese, eggs, and omelets.

Compared to table salt, are "natural" salts healthier?
   In salt mines or by evaporating ocean water, salt is produced. Sodium chloride is the main component of all salts, and each kind of salt has about the same nutritional content. Some minerals are in less processed salts but only in minute quantities. The fundamental reason for choosing

various salts is taste. The most popular kind, table salt, is taken from salt deposits under the earth. It undergoes extensive processing to eliminate contaminants, which might also eliminate trace minerals. Then it is finely ground.

In 1924, iodine, a trace mineral, was added to salt to prevent the medical conditions of goiter and hypothyroidism caused by an iodine shortage. To avoid clumping, table salt is often combined with an anti-caking ingredient like calcium silicate. Kosher salt is a coarse-grained salt that gets its name from being used to prepare traditional Kosher meals. Although iodine is normally absent from kosher salt, it could include an anti-caking ingredient.

Ocean or sea water is evaporated to create sea salt. It mainly consists of sodium chloride, but depending on where it was gathered, it may also include trace levels of minerals, including potassium, zinc, and iron. It may look rougher and darker with an uneven hue since it is not as well-refined and powdered as table salt, suggesting that there are still nutrients and contaminants. Sadly, some of these contaminants may include lead or other oceanic metals. Brands will differ in terms of granule size and coarseness.

Pakistani mines are used to collect Himalayan pink salt, and trace levels of iron oxide cause its pink color. It is similar to sea salt in that it has had less processing and refinement, giving the crystals a bigger appearance and a few trace levels of minerals, including iron, calcium, potassium, and magnesium. Larger, coarser salt granules provide a flavorful kick but may dissolve slowly and evenly in cooking. It is best to sprinkle them over meats and vegetables before or after cooking. The use of them in baking recipes is not advised.

Remember that various salts' measurements are sometimes interchangeable in recipes. If the granule size is comparable, sea salt and table salt may often be used interchangeably. One teaspoon of table salt may be substituted for 1.5 to 2 teaspoons of kosher salt, depending on the brand, since table salt has a more concentrated, saltier taste than kosher salt.

The interaction between sodium and potassium

Although sodium and potassium are closely related, their effects on the body are opposed. Both are vital nutrients essential for maintaining physiological equilibrium and have been associated with an increased risk of chronic illnesses, including cardiovascular disease. Excessive potassium consumption may assist in relaxing blood vessels and help the body eliminate sodium while lowering blood pressure.

However, a diet heavy in salt increases blood pressure and may lead to cardiovascular disease. Every day, our bodies need considerably more potassium than salt. Yet, the average American diet does the exact opposite: Americans' typical daily salt intake is 3,300 milligrams, 75% of which comes from processed foods, but only 2,900 milligrams of potassium.

Journal of Internal Medicine reports that:

- Diets rich in sodium and deficient in potassium increase the risk of death from heart attacks and other causes in people. In this research, those who consumed the most salt had a 20% greater chance of passing away from any cause than those who consumed the least sodium. The risk of death was 20% lower for those with higher potassium intakes than those with lower intakes. However, the diet's link between sodium and potassium may be even more crucial for health. People who consumed more sodium than potassium in their diets had a 50% greater risk of dying from any cause and a twofold increased chance of dying from a heart attack.

- One necessary dietary modification that people may do to reduce their risk is to consume more fresh produce, which is naturally rich in potassium and low in sodium, and less bread, cheese, processed meat, and other processed foods, which are low in potassium and high in sodium.

What Does Hypernatremia Mean?

The medical word for having too much salt in your blood is hypernatremia. One of the body's electrolytes, sodium, which is mostly contained in blood, is crucial for numerous biological processes. However, an electrolyte imbalance might develop if there is an overabundance.

Hypernatremia: an excess of sodium

Hypernatremia occurs when the blood's sodium and water levels are abnormal, leading to either excess sodium or a water deficiency. This may happen when the body gains (or accumulates) too much salt or loses too much water. A reading above 145 milliequivalents per liter is called hypernatremia by medical professionals; a typical range is between 136 and 145 milliequivalents per liter.

The brain naturally regulates the quantity of salt and water in your body in healthy individuals by balancing intake and outflow, such as becoming thirsty or peeing. Your kidneys may eliminate more salt from your circulation if your brain notices that your body's levels are too high. Your brain can also induce thirst to encourage you to drink water.

Dehydration is often a sign of hypernatremia. Most instances of moderate hypernatremia may be treated by rehydrating if dehydration is the cause. A person usually detects minor hypernatremia when they feel thirsty and dehydrated, and they treat it by drinking water or an elec-trolyte-rich sports drink. However, milder instances could also need medical attention.

Hypernatremia symptoms include:

- muscle sluggishness
- restlessness
- severe thirst
- confusion
- lethargy
- irritability
- seizures
- Unconsciousness

Particularly in young children, hypernatremia may be quite dangerous. It may bring on dehydration, vomiting, diarrhea, profuse sweating, severe burns, or other underlying health issues. Similar to hyponatremia, hypernatremia in the elderly may lead to extremely significant issues. Sometimes as we age, our brains become less sensitive to electrolyte imbalances, which may result in excess sodium in the blood. Kidney issues in older individuals are another factor that might cause hypernatremia.

Treatment and Diagnosis of Hypernatremia

A blood test may be used to determine the presence of hypernatremia. Urine testing may also be used sometimes. Treating hypernatremia aims to restore your body's optimal salt and fluid balance. Your doctor will probably use an IV to replenish the fluids in your body if your hypernatremia is more severe than moderate. This will immediately deliver fluids into your bloodstream, balancing the quantity of salt already there.

Hypernatremia is often treatable. However, to ensure that there aren't any more issues with your brain or kidneys that need treatment, your doctor will want to identify the underlying cause of your hypernatremia.

Hypernatremia-related complications

A cerebral blood artery rupture is one of the most severe effects of hypernatremia. This bleeding in the brain, also known as a subarachnoid or subdural hemorrhage, may result in lasting brain damage or even death. Suppose doctors can diagnose hypernatremia early and begin treatment to restore the body's salt and water balance. They may prevent severe complications, including brain damage, seizures, and death.

Methods for Avoiding Hypernatremia

The simplest method to avoid hypernatremia is to ensure you are well-hydrated and take sufficient salt. According to recommendations, the typical adult should have four to six glasses of water daily. To prevent dehydration and hypernatremia, you should drink more if you are taking certain drugs, particularly active, in a hot environment, or at a high altitude.

According to the American Heart Association, an optimum salt intake for a healthy adult is 1,500 milligrams per day. According to the group, the average daily consumption for Americans is above 3,400 milligrams, which may lead to major health issues, including hypernatremia and other imbalances. The AHA advises avoiding processed foods and restaurant meals in favor of home-cooked meals and monitoring salt consumption. Most individuals should be able to prevent hypernatremia with a healthy, balanced diet and enough fluids. However, an electrolyte imbalance brought on by other disorders might lead to hypernatremia. It is a medical emergency in this instance, which physicians can handle.

Hyponatremia

Hyponatremia is characterized by a dangerously low sodium level in the blood. As an electrolyte, sodium aids in controlling the volume of water in and around your cells. When you have hyponatremia, your body's sodium levels are diluted for one or more reasons, such as an underlying medical condition or too much water. Your body's water content increases, and your cells start to inflate. From minor to potentially fatal health issues, this swelling may be the source of numerous. The goal of treating hyponatremia is to address the underlying problem. Depending on what caused the hyponatremia, you may need to drink less, and you could need intravenous electrolyte solutions and drugs in other hyponatremia instances.

Symptoms

Signs and symptoms of hyponatremia might include:

- vomiting and nauseous
- headache
- confusion
- low energy, weariness, and sleepiness
- anxiety and restlessness
- weakness, cramps, or muscle spasms
- seizures
- Coma

When to see a doctor

Anyone experiencing severe hyponatremia symptoms, such as nausea, vomiting, disorientation, seizures, or loss of consciousness, should seek immediate medical attention. Call your doctor immediately if you are at risk for hyponatremia and suffer nausea, headaches, cramps, or weakness. Your doctor may advise getting emergency medical attention based on the severity and length of these symptoms.

Hyponatremia may result from a wide range of medical disorders and lifestyle choices, including:

- Specific medicines. Some drugs, such as diuretics, painkillers, and antidepressants, may interfere with the hormone and renal functions that regulate salt levels within a healthy normal range.
- Issues with the liver, kidneys, and heart. When fluids build up in your body due to conditions like congestive heart failure or ailments of the kidneys or liver, the general amount of sodium in your body is lowered.
- Inappropriate antidiuretic hormone syndrome (SIADH). High quantities of the antidiuretic hormone (ADH) are generated in this disease, causing your body to retain water rather than expel it regularly via your urine.
- Prolonged, severe diarrhea or vomiting and other dehydration-causing factors. This raises levels of ADH while also causing your body to lose electrolytes like salt.
- Abusing the water supply. Low sodium levels may result from excessive water intake since it overwhelms the kidneys' capacity to eliminate water. Drinking too much water during endurance events like marathons and triathlons may also lower the salt level in your blood because you lose sodium via perspiration.
- Changes in hormones. Your adrenal glands' capacity to generate hormones that support the maintenance of your body's salt, potassium and water balance is impacted by adrenal gland

insufficiency (Addison's disease). Low thyroid hormone levels may also bring on low blood sodium levels.

- Ecstasy is a substance used for fun. This amphetamine increases the likelihood of developing severe or even catastrophic hyponatremia.

Risk factors

The following variables may increase your risk of hyponatremia:

- Age. Older people may be more susceptible to hyponatremia due to aging-related changes, drugs, and a higher risk of chronic illness affecting the body's salt balance.
- Certain drugs. Thiazide diuretics, several antidepressants, and some painkillers are among the drugs that raise your risk of hyponatremia. Ecstasy, a popular drug, has also been connected to fatal hyponatremia instances.
- Illnesses that cause your body to excrete less water. Kidney disease, inappropriate antidiuretic hormone (SIADH) syndrome, heart failure, and other illnesses may all raise your risk of hyponatremia.
- Vigorous physical activity. A higher risk of hyponatremia exists in those who overhydrate when participating in marathons, ultramarathons, triathlons, and other long-distance, high-intensity events.

Complications

Chronic hyponatremia is characterized by a slow decline in sodium levels over 48 hours, with milder symptoms and effects. Sodium levels decrease quickly in acute hyponatremia, which may have potentially harmful implications, such as rapid brain swelling that might cause a coma and death. Women in their premenopausal years seem to be most susceptible to brain damage brought on by hyponatremia. This could be connected to how women's sex hormones affect the body's capacity to maintain healthy salt levels.

Prevention

The following steps might assist you in avoiding hyponatremia:

- Manage comorbid conditions. Treatment for illnesses like adrenal gland insufficiency, which causes hyponatremia, may help avoid low blood salt levels.
- Inform yourself. You should be aware of the signs and symptoms of hyponatremia if you have a medical condition that makes you more prone to it or if you use diuretic medicines. Always discuss the dangers of a new medicine with your doctor.
- Use care while engaging in vigorous activity. During a race, athletes should only consume as many liquids as they sweat off. The amount of water or other fluids you require may be determined by your thirst.

- When engaging in strenuous activities, think about consuming sports drinks. If you want to participate in endurance sports like marathons, triathlons, or other strenuous activities, talk to your doctor about substituting water with drinks that include electrolytes.
- Drink water sparingly. Getting adequate fluids is vital for your health, so drink enough water. But don't go overboard. The most excellent indicators of how much water you need are typically thirst and the color of your urine. If your pee is light yellow and you are not dehydrated, you should consume enough water.

Diagnosis

In the first step of the process, your doctor will do a thorough medical history interview and physical examination. However, a physical exam alone cannot identify hyponatremia since the signs and symptoms may also be seen in various other illnesses. Your doctor will request blood testing and urine tests to confirm low blood sodium levels.

Treatment

If at all feasible, the therapy for hyponatremia is to address the underlying cause.

Your doctor could advise temporarily reducing fluid intake if you have mild, persistent hyponatremia brought on by your diet, prescription medications, or overconsumption of water. They can also advise modifying how often you take diuretics to raise the amount of salt in your blood. You will need more active therapy if you have severe, acute hyponatremia. Options consist of:

- Intravenous fluids. To gradually increase the salt levels in your blood, your doctor could suggest an IV sodium solution. This necessitates a hospital stay for ongoing salt level monitoring since correcting too quickly might be harmful.
- Medications. You may take medication to treat the signs and symptoms of hyponatremia, such as headaches, nausea, and seizures.

Getting ready for the appointment

Anyone experiencing severe hyponatremia symptoms, such as nausea, vomiting, disorientation, seizures, or loss of consciousness, should seek immediate medical attention. Call your doctor immediately if you are at risk for hyponatremia and suffer nausea, headaches, cramps, or weakness. Your doctor may advise getting emergency medical attention based on the severity and length of these symptoms. Here is some information to help you prepare for your visit and what to anticipate from your doctor if you have the time.

How can you provide information?

- Indicate any symptoms you or a loved one have been having, along with when they started.
- List any drugs, vitamins, supplements, and other natural remedies you are taking and any other medical conditions for which you are receiving treatment.

- Bring a loved one or friend with you if you go to the hospital because of low blood salt. If you have company, they can help you recall everything and assist you if you need emergency medical attention.
- You should compile a list of questions to ask your physician.

Some fundamental inquiries to make of your doctor about hyponatremia are:

What is the most probable reason for my symptoms?

- What brings about hyponatremia?
- How serious is the illness?
- What course of action do you suggest?
- When do you anticipate that my symptoms will start to get better?
- Am I susceptible to any long-term issues?
- How can I stop this issue from recurring?
- Do I need to alter the number of liquids I typically consume?

What to anticipate from your physician

Being prepared to respond to your doctor's inquiries allows you to reserve time to review any topics you wish to discuss in further detail.

Your doctor could query the following:

- What symptoms do you have, and when did they start?
- Do you currently use any new medications?
- Have your symptoms improved or become worse since they started?
- Have any mental changes, such as feeling disoriented, irritated, or sad, been a part of your symptoms?
- Have you had diarrhea, vomiting, or nausea?
- Have you experienced dizziness, convulsions, or loss of consciousness?
- Have you had a headache? If so, has it become worse over time?
- Have you experienced weakness, weariness, or sluggishness as symptoms?
- Do you take drugs recreationally? If so, which medicines?

Final Thoughts

The body's water is contained in three compartments: fluid within and around cells and blood: Electrolytes, especially sodium, aid in maintaining appropriate fluid levels. Hypernatremia, hyponatremia, and hypokalemia are all life-threatening conditions that may result from excessive or inadequate sodium and potassium levels. Sodium is essential for healthy neuron and muscle function, and the body loses salt through sweat and urine.

. . .

Guidelines for Appropriate Intakes (AI) and Chronic Disease Risk Reduction (CDRR) intakes are recommended, but most Americans eat more salt than is recommended. Sodium is a nutrient found in many foods, such as bread and rolls, pizza, sandwiches, cold cuts and cured meats, soups, burritos, tacos, savory snacks, chicken, cheese, eggs, and omelets. Hypernatremia is an abnormality in the blood's sodium and water levels, leading to either an excess of sodium or a water deficiency. It can be caused by dehydration, vomiting, diarrhea, profuse sweating, severe burns, or other underlying health issues. To avoid hypernatremia, it is important to be well-hydrated and take in a sufficient amount of salt. Treatment aims to restore the body's optimal salt and fluid balance. Prevention includes managing comorbid conditions and informing oneself of the signs and symptoms.

The key features in this chapter:

- The weight of the body is mainly made up of water.
- According to medical professionals, the body's water is contained in several fluid compartments.
- Maintaining a fluid balance between the compartments requires having electrolytes in the proper concentrations (electrolyte balance).
- Disorders may arise if the electrolyte balance is off.
- They're also an essential part of making a diagnosis for a variety of illnesses and ailments.

2

SODIUM AND HEALTH

The kidneys often struggle to handle too much salt in the blood, and the body hangs onto the water to hydrate itself when sodium builds up. As a result, more fluid flows around cells, and blood flows through the circulation. A larger amount of blood strains the heart and the blood arteries. The additional strain and pressure over time may harden blood vessels, increasing the risk of hypertension, heart attacks, and stroke. Heart failure may result from it. There is some proof that overeating salt may harm your bones and your heart, aorta, and kidneys without raising your blood pressure.

Cardiovascular disease

The Institute of Medicine concluded that lowering salt consumption decreases blood pressure, despite conflicting data about a reduced risk of cardiovascular diseases (CVD). But it is undeniable that CVD has a high blood pressure component, and it causes half of the heart disease and two-thirds of all strokes. More than one million fatalities annually in China are attributable to high blood pressure, the leading avoidable cause of mortality. People react differently to decreased sodium intakes, suggesting that salt consumption may have a hereditary component. The most significant blood pressure drops occur in those who are "salt-sensitive" after following a diet low in sodium. " salt-resistant " people do not notice these effects even when their sodium consumption significantly increases.

According to studies, individuals who react best to decreased salt consumption are more likely to be female than male, older than 50, African-American, and those with higher baseline blood pressure. Although the ideal goal level is not apparent, the overall data suggest a benefit of restricting sodium consumption for everyone, even if there needs to be more information to draw firm judgments regarding particular individuals that may be salt-resistant. Observations and clinical studies show that higher salt intake is linked to cardiovascular illnesses and fatalities. These are essential studies:

- Intersalt: Scientists studied sodium excretion over 24 hours in more than 10,000 persons from 32 nations (a decent proxy for salt consumption). The typical daily salt intake was close to 4,000 mg. The difference was nevertheless significant, ranging from 200 mg per day among the Yanomamo people of Brazil to 10,300 mg in northern Japan. Average and age-related blood pressure rises were higher in populations with more salt. Four populations—four nations with salt consumption below 1,300 mg daily—had low average blood pressures and little to no aging-related increase in blood pressure.

The Intersalt data underwent a review and update by the authors. They discovered: 1) a larger link between higher salt intakes and higher blood pressure than they had previously seen; and 2) a stronger correlation between middle-aged individuals' blood pressure levels and those of younger persons.

- TOHP: From 1987 to 1995, two Trials of Hypertension Prevention (TOHP) were undertaken. They investigated the effects of modifying one's lifestyle, including reducing salt intake, managing stress, losing weight, and managing stress. With a salt reduction over 18–36 months, modest drops in blood pressure were seen in each study. The researchers surveyed the subjects after the trials had concluded, and they discovered:
- The TOHP individuals in the sodium-reduction groups had a 25% lower risk of dying from cardiovascular disease, having a heart attack, or needing surgery to open or bypass a coronary artery that had become blocked with cholesterol after an average of 10-15 years.
- The risk of acquiring cardiovascular disease decreased with a participant's diet's potassium to sodium ratio. This shows that the best way to treat high blood pressure is to raise potassium levels and reduce salt levels.
- TOHP Follow-up Study: A follow-up to the two TOHP investigations on cardiovascular disease

and death rates completed in 2000. There was a 32% decreased risk of CVD among those with less than 2,300 mg of salt daily compared to those with 3,600–4,800 mg. Furthermore, with lowering salt intakes as low as 1,500 mg per day, CVD-related events (stroke, heart attack) continued to decline.

- DASH: In 1994, the Dietary Approaches to Stop Hypertension (DASH) trials provided groundbreaking evidence between diet and hypertension.

- In the first trial, 459 people were randomized to one of three diets: the "DASH diet," which prioritized fruits, vegetables, and low-fat dairy foods while limiting red meat, saturated fats, and sweets. The other two diets were comparable but higher in fruits and vegetables. After eight weeks, the fruits and vegetable diet and the DASH diet, with the DASH diet having a more significant impact, decreased systolic (the top number on a blood pressure measurement) and diastolic (the bottom number on a blood pressure reading).

In the second trial, it was shown that decreasing salt in either the DASH diet or the typical American diet significantly lowered blood pressure. The Dietary Guidelines for Americans 2010, which advice limiting daily salt intake to less than a teaspoon, are primarily supported by research from the DASH trial. According to a meta-analysis of clinical studies, people with both regular and high blood pressure saw substantial drops in their blood pressure when their salt intake was moderately reduced to about 4,000 mg per day for at least one month.

Further investigation revealed that both men and women and people of both white and black races had lower blood pressure, indicating a benefit for the general populace. It might be challenging to gauge someone's salt consumption, but the most precise way currently available is to collect 24 urine samples over a few days. Data from six prospective cohorts, including the Nurses Health Studies I and II, the Health Professionals Follow-up Study, the Prevention of Renal and Vascular End-Stage Disease study, and the Trials of Hypertension Prevention Follow-up studies involving 10,709 otherwise healthy adults, were pooled by Harvard researchers using this technique.

Each person provided at least two urine samples. They looked at sodium and potassium intakes concerning the risk of cardiovascular disease (CVD) (as indicated by a heart attack, stroke, or procedure or surgery required to repair heart damage). They discovered that greater salt consumption was linked to a higher chance of developing CVD after adjusting for CVD risk variables. There was an 18% higher risk of CVD for every 1,000 mg rise in urine salt per day. But the incidence of CVD decreased by 18% for every 1,000 mg increase in potassium. Additionally, they discovered that consuming more salty foods than potassium-rich foods such as fruits, vegetables, legumes, and low-fat dairy products were linked to an increased risk of CVD.

Chronic kidney disease

Strong evidence links high blood pressure to CKD and cardiovascular disease exists. According to reports, salt sensitivity is more common in CKD patients because of a decreased capacity to eliminate sodium, which might cause blood pressure to rise.

A modest sodium limitation does not adequately protect against or improve the outcomes of CKD compared to a moderate sodium restriction, despite evidence linking excessive sodium consumption with high blood pressure.

According to a systematic study of CKD patients, low sodium intakes of less than 2,300 mg per day showed no discernible impact compared to moderate sodium intakes of 2,300–4,600 mg per day. However, high sodium intakes of more than 4,600 mg per day were linked to the advancement of CKD.

Most recommendations recommend a moderate rather than a low sodium restriction to stop the onset and progression of CKD. It is recommended to consume less sodium daily than 4,000 mg for managing CKD overall and less sodium than 3,000 mg for CKD with symptoms of fluid retention or proteinuria, in which too much protein is excreted in the urine.

Osteoporosis

Your body excretes more calcium through urine the more salt you eat. Calcium may leak out of bones if not enough is in the blood. In light of this, osteoporosis, a condition that causes the weakening of the bones, may also be a side effect of a high-sodium diet. In a study of postmenopausal women, the relationship between bone loss and 24-hour urine salt excretion at the beginning of the trial was as significant as the relationship between calcium consumption and bone loss. Other research has shown that cutting down on salt results in a positive calcium balance, which raises the possibility that doing so might decrease the aging-related loss of calcium from bones.

Cancer

According to research, more salt, sodium, or salty meals may increase your risk of developing stomach cancer. Both the American Institute for Cancer Research and the World Cancer Research Fund cite salt and other salted or salty foods as "probable causes" of stomach cancer.

Signs of Toxicity and Deficiency

Deficiency

Because salt is often added to a broad range of meals and is present naturally in certain foods, sodium deficiencies are uncommon in the United States. This often affects older adults, especially those residing in nursing homes or hospitals, who take drugs or have medical disorders that cause the body to lose salt, resulting in hyponatremia.

Hyponatremia may also result from excessive sweating, vomiting, or diarrhea if salt is lost in these bodily fluids. Hyponatremia may sometimes result from too much fluid abnormally accumulating in the body; conditions like heart failure or liver cirrhosis may cause this. Rarely, merely consuming too much fluid might cause hyponatremia if the kidneys cannot eliminate the extra water. Hyponatremia symptoms might include headaches, nausea, vomiting, altered mental status/confusion, lethargy, seizures, and coma.

Toxicity

An excess of sodium in the blood may strike older persons who are physically and intellectually disabled, undereat or overhydrated, or ill with an infection that causes extreme dehydration or a high fever. Other factors include diuretic drugs that cause the body to lose water or excessive perspiration. Water is moved from cells into the blood to dilute it when sodium builds up in circulation. Seizures, comas, and even death may result from this fluid shift and fluid buildup in the brain. Breathing difficulties may be brought on by extra fluid accumulating in the lungs. Hypernatremia may also cause renal damage, weakness, nausea, vomiting, lack of appetite, extreme thirst, and nausea.

What Is the Recommended Daily Intake of Sodium?

Minerals like sodium are essential. To avoid diseases like high blood pressure, health organizations advise healthy persons to keep their daily sodium consumption to less than 2,300 mg (about one teaspoon of salt). Nearly all of the foods and beverages you consume include sodium, which is sometimes just referred to as salt. It is present naturally in various foods, added to others during production, and used in restaurants and at home as a flavoring ingredient.

Sodium has long been associated with high blood pressure, which harms your arteries and blood vessels when kept at a sustained high level. Your chance of developing heart disease, stroke, heart failure, and renal disease rises. Therefore, several health organizations have made recommendations for reducing salt consumption. However, these recommendations have generated debate since not everyone will benefit from a diet low in salt. The significance of sodium, possible hazards of over- or under-consumption, and the recommended daily sodium intake are all covered in this section.

Required for Health

Despite ongoing criticism, salt is an essential mineral for wellness. It's one among the minerals called electrolytes that your body uses to produce electrically charged ions. Sodium chloride, the common table salt, has 40% sodium and 60% chloride by weight and significantly contributes to the sodium content of most people's diets. Since salt is often utilized in the production and processing of food, processed meals are thought to be the source of 75% of all sodium intake.

Blood and the fluid surrounding your cells contain most of your body's salt, and sodium plays a role in keeping these fluids in balance. In addition to maintaining a regular fluid balance, sodium is essential for healthy neuron and muscle activity.

By changing the quantity of sodium expelled in urine, your kidneys aid in controlling the amount of sodium in your body. Sweating also causes salt loss. Even with deficient sodium diets, dietary sodium shortages are uncommon daily.

Associated with high blood pressure

It has long been known that salt raises blood pressure, especially in those with high amounts. Most experts agree that France was the first country to discover the connection between salt and high blood pressure in 1904. Even yet, this association was generally acknowledged when the scientist

Walter Kempner showed that a low-salt rice diet might drop blood pressure in 500 persons with high levels in the late 1940s. Since then, research has shown a solid link between consuming too much salt and having high blood pressure.

The Prospective Urban Rural Epidemiology experiment, or PURE, is one of the most prominent studies on this subject. Researchers examined the salt levels in the urine of more than 100,000 individuals from 18 nations on five continents. They discovered that those with greater sodium intakes had considerably higher blood pressure than those with lower intakes. Using the same sample, other researchers showed that those who drank more than 7 grams of salt daily had a greater chance of developing heart disease and dying young than those who ingested 3-6 grams daily.

Not everyone, however, reacts to salt in the same manner. The effects of salt on blood pressure tend to be more noticeable in those with high blood pressure, diabetes, chronic renal disease, older folks, and African Americans. Limiting sodium consumption is advised if you are sensitive to salt since you may be more likely to develop heart disease linked to high blood pressure.

Official Dietary Advice

Health experts have long advised individuals to consume less salt to lower blood pressure. According to estimates, your body only requires 186 mg of salt daily. However, eating this little and acquiring the required amounts of other crucial nutrients would take much work. To prevent this, the Institute of Medicine (IOM) advises healthy persons to eat 1,500 mg (1.5 grams) of salt daily.

. . .

The Institute of Medicine and the United States Department of Agriculture advise that the average healthy individual consume no more than 2,300 milligrams (2.3 grams), or approximately one teaspoon of salt, daily. This upper limit was set based on data from clinical research showing that daily salt intakes exceeding 2,300 mg (2.3 grams) might negatively influence blood pressure and raise the risk of heart disease.

Due to the higher salt loss via sweat, these recommendations only apply to some active persons, such as competitive athletes or outdoor laborers, the groups making different suggestions. The American Heart Association recommends a considerably lower consumption of 1,500 mg (1.5 grams) of salt than the WHO's 2,000 mg (2 grams) daily. Americans eat roughly 3,400 mg (3.4 grams) of salt daily, far higher than health professionals advise.

Meanwhile, these suggestions have generated debate since limiting salt consumption may not benefit those with normal blood pressure. According to the available research, less salt consumption does not reduce the risk of heart disease in healthy individuals and may even be dangerous.

Dangers of Underconsumption

According to some research, reducing salt consumption to the recommended amounts may be detrimental. Researchers looked at how salt consumption influenced the risk of heart disease and early mortality in a review study that included more than 133,000 participants with and without high blood pressure from 49 countries on six continents.

Regardless of blood pressure, the research found that those who drank less than 3,000 mg (3 grams) of salt daily had a higher risk of developing heart disease or passing away than those who consumed 4,000–5,000 mg (4–5 grams). Additionally, individuals who ingested less salt than 3,000 mg (3 grams) had lower health results than those who consumed 7,000 mg (7 grams).

Heart disease or death risk was considerably higher in high blood pressure patients who ingested more than 7 grams of salt per day than those who consumed 4-5 grams. These and other findings imply that lower salt intakes may be more harmful to people's health than higher ones.

Should you limit what you eat?

More than 7 grams of salt daily is too much for those with high blood pressure. Therefore they should limit their intake. The same may be true if your doctor or registered dietitian has advised you to reduce your salt consumption for health reasons, as in the case of a low-sodium therapeutic diet. However, reducing salt intake has little impact on healthy individuals.

Although health officials continue to advocate for decreased salt diets, going below 3 grams daily may harm health. According to studies, persons who drink less than 3 grams of daily salt risk developing heart disease and dying young than those who ingest 4-5 grams. An increasing body of research indicates that the existing sodium limits, which range from 1,500 mg (1.5 grams) to 2,300 mg (2.3 grams), may be too low, raising questions about whether they are beneficial. However, the amount of healthy salt individuals take is generally safe, with just 22% of the population from 49 nations consuming more than 6 grams of sodium daily.

. . .

Final Thoughts

Reducing salt consumption decreases blood pressure, but CVD has a high blood pressure component. Salt-resistant individuals are more likely to be female than male, older than 50, African-American, and those with higher baseline blood pressure.

The TOHP and DASH trials demonstrated that lowering salt intake and increasing potassium levels are the most effective ways to treat high blood pressure. Decreasing salt intake had a more significant effect on lowering blood pressure, with both men and women and people of both white and black races having lower blood pressure. High blood pressure, osteoporosis, and stomach cancer are all linked to a high-sodium diet.

Hyponatremia is an acute disease caused by low sodium levels in the blood, which can cause headaches, nausea, vomiting, altered mental status/confusion, lethargy, seizures, and coma.

Sodium is an essential mineral for health, but it has been linked to high blood pressure, heart disease, stroke, heart failure, and renal disease. Salt has been linked to high blood pressure, especially in those with high amounts, and the Institute of Medicine and the US Department of Agriculture advise no more than 2,300 milligrams (2.3 grams) daily. Reducing salt consumption may not reduce the risk of heart disease in healthy individuals and may even be dangerous. Reducing salt intake may harm health, but it is generally safe.

The key features in this chapter

- The kidneys often struggle to handle too much salt in the blood.
- People who are "salt-resistant" do not notice these effects even when their sodium consumption significantly increases.
- Average blood pressure and age-related blood pressure rises were higher in populations with more salt.
- Chronic kidney disease There is strong evidence linking high blood pressure to CKD and cardiovascular disease.
- Cancer According to research, consuming more salt, sodium, or salty meals is associated with increased stomach cancer.
- Toxicity Hypernatremia refers to an excess of sodium in the blood.
- Required for health Despite ongoing criticism, salt is essential for wellness.
- According to the available research, less salt consumption does not reduce the risk of heart disease in healthy individuals.
- Reducing salt intake has little impact on healthy individuals.

3

SODIUM IN YOUR DIET

Reduce your consumption by using the nutrition facts label. You've likely heard that most Americans consume too much salt. A limited amount of sodium is necessary for your body to function correctly, but too much salt may harm your health. Higher salt diets are linked to an increased risk of high blood pressure, a key contributor to heart disease and stroke.

Contrary to what many believe, consuming packaged and prepared foods—rather than adding table salt to meals while cooking or eating—provides the majority of dietary sodium (over 70%). Americans who wish to eat less salt may find it challenging since the food supply already contains too much. Because of this, the FDA is working with the food industry to decrease salt in various foods reasonably and equitably. Although many packaged items may already include salt when you buy them, you may reduce your daily sodium consumption by consulting the Nutrition Facts label.

Look at the Label!

Utilize the Nutrition Facts label as a tool to help you decide!

- Be aware of Daily Value. The Daily Values are recommended nutritional intake levels that should not exceed daily. Less than 2,300 milligrams (mg) of salt are included in the Daily Value (DV) per day.
- Make use of the % Daily Value (%DV) tool. Percent Daily Value (%DV) expresses the proportion of the Daily Value (DV) for a nutrient that can be expected to be provided by a single serving of food or drink. Use %DV to compare foods that consume less sodium than 100% DV each day and evaluate if a portion of a meal is high or low in sodium. Generally, a sodium content of 5% DV or less is considered low, whereas a sodium content of 20% DV or more is considered high.
- Pay close attention to portions. The Nutrition Facts label typically contains the nutritional data for one product serving. To determine how much sodium you ingest, look at the serving size and quantity you consume.

Food Choices Matter!

The following foods make up approximately 40% of the salt Americans eat, according to the Centers for Disease Control and Prevention (CDC):

- Deli sandwiches with meat

- Pizza
- Tacos and burritos
- Soups
- Favorite Snacks (e.g., chips, crackers, popcorn)
- Poultry
- Mixed pasta dishes
- Burgers
- Omelets and other egg dishes

But keep in mind that comparable kinds of meals might have considerably different salt contents. To compare items accurately, utilize the Nutrition Facts label and remember to look at the serving size.

Sodium as an Ingredient in Food

Sodium serves various purposes as a food component, including meat curing, baking, thickening, preserving moisture, boosting taste (including the flavor of other ingredients), and serving as a preservative. Several popular food additives, including sodium-containing monosodium glutamate (MSG), sodium bicarbonate (baking soda), sodium nitrite, and sodium benzoate, are labeled as having "sodium" in their total quantities on the Nutrition Facts label.

Surprisingly, certain meals that don't taste salty may be high in sodium; thus, relying only on taste to determine a food's sodium level must be more accurate. For instance, many meals (such as cereals and pastries) contain sodium but don't taste salty, unlike those rich in sodium (such as pickles and soy sauce), which have a salty flavor. Additionally, while some foods (such as bread) may not be very rich in sodium, eating them often throughout the day might result in a significant daily salt intake.

Check for nutritional claims on the package

To rapidly find foods and drinks that could have less sodium, you can also look for nutritional claims on the packaging of such items. Here is a list of typical assertions and what they mean:

What It Says and What It Means

Salt/Sodium-Free
Less than 5 mg of sodium per serving

Very low sodium
35 mg of sodium or less per serving

Low Sodium
140 mg of sodium or less per serving

Reduced Sodium
At least 25% less sodium than the regular product

Light in sodium or lightly salted
At least 50% less sodium than the regular product

No-Salt-Added or Unsalted

No salt is added during processing – but these products may not be salt/sodium-free unless stated.

Sodium and Blood Pressure

A high-sodium diet pulls water into circulation because sodium attracts water, which may raise blood pressure by increasing blood volume. High blood pressure, often known as hypertension, is a chronic condition characterized by a persistently high blood pressure reading over time. Since hypertension forces the heart to work too hard, high blood pressure may damage organs and arteries (such as the heart, kidneys, brain, and eyes). Renal illness, blindness, heart attack, heart failure, and stroke become more likely when high blood pressure is not managed. Limiting salt consumption becomes crucial yearly since it usually increases as you age.

Know Your Numbers

Sodium is an essential component that the body needs in tiny quantities to keep bodily fluids in balance, keep muscles and nerves functioning properly, and prevent excessive perspiration. An average American consumes 3,400 mg of salt daily. However, the Dietary Guidelines for Americans advise individuals to keep their daily sodium consumption to under 2,300 mg, roughly one teaspoon of table salt. Recommended upper limits are much lower for kids under the age of 14.

10 Simple strategies to cut your sodium intake

You may reduce your sodium intake by learning about the amount of sodium in different meals and using new food preparation techniques. Additionally, if you use these recommendations to reduce your salt intake, you may not notice a difference in how you feel about it.

Read the nutrition information label, To consume less than the DV (less than 2,300 mg) of salt daily, compare and choose foods.

Whenever you can, make your own meals. Reduce the number of boxed sauces, mixes, and "instant" goods (including flavored rice, instant noodles, and ready-made pasta).

Without increasing salt, increase the taste. When cooking, baking, or eating, keep the quantity of table salt you need to season food to a minimum. Instead of salt, experiment with no-salt seasoning mixes, herbs, and spices to flavor your cuisine.

Buy fresh. Avoid processed meats and go for fresh meat, poultry, and seafood. Look at fresh meat and poultry packaging to detect whether salt water or saline has been added.

Observe your vegetables. Purchase fresh, frozen veggies that aren't seasoned or sauced, reduced sodium, or salt-free canned vegetables.

"Rinse" sodium with water. Before eating, rinse canned items such as beans, tuna, and salads containing salt. This helps to reduce sodium.

Your snacks are "unsalted.". Pick nuts, seeds, and snack foods (such as chips and pretzels) with minimal or no salt added, or go for carrot or celery sticks.

Think about your condiments. Condiments may contain a lot of sodium. Pick condiments with no salt content, dress salads with oil and vinegar rather than bottled dressings, and season food with flavoring packets sparingly rather than using the full package.

Eat fewer portions. Less sodium implies less food. When dining out, order smaller servings, share an entrée with a buddy, or take some of your meal homes. You may also prepare smaller portions at home and consume less food overall.

Reduce your salt intake while dining out. Request that table salt is omitted from your meal, and ask for sauces and salad dressings to be given "on the side" so you may use less. If nutrition information is available, you may also request it and then choose choices with less salt.

Facts regarding sodium intake and our food supply

- Consuming less than 2,300 milligrams (mg) of salt daily is recommended by the 2020-2025 Dietary Guidelines for Americans.
- Nearly 90% of Americans aged two and older overindulge in sodium.
- Americans aged two and older consume more than 3,400 mg of salt daily.
- Americans now consume much more salt than they did in the 1970s. Since 2010, several manufacturers have cut the salt content of various goods, and some demographic groups have seen a minor decline in sodium intake.
- Processed and restaurant foods account for around 70% of daily salt intake. Salt and sodium

are only used in tiny amounts in cooking and at the table.

- Even highly motivated individuals may find it challenging to lower their salt consumption since manufactured, and restaurant items already include sodium when bought.
- Different brands of the same sorts of meals may have different sodium contents. A serving of a fast-food cheeseburger might contain anywhere from 710 milligrams to 1,690 milligrams of salt. In contrast, a single serving of frozen pizza cheese may have anywhere from 370 milligrams to 730 milligrams of salt.
- It might be challenging for consumers to estimate sodium levels since the information is not always easily accessible for prepared or restaurant items.

Sodium reduction and burden reduction for cardiovascular disease

- Reduction of high blood pressure lowers the risk of developing heart disease and stroke. Adults with raised and high blood pressure benefit, particularly from lowering blood pressure.
- Public salt intake may be decreased to safety levels if manufacturers progressively lower the quantity of sodium in prepared and processed foods, with little to no change in consumer behavior.
- High hypertension, heart attacks, and stroke are attributed to sodium consumption from

processed and restaurant meals. Reducing salt consumption might save thousands of lives yearly since high blood pressure is a factor in roughly 500,000 fatalities annually.

- By lowering salt consumption to 2,300 mg daily, the specific population might save $18 billion on medical expenses and avert 11 million instances of hypertension each year.
- Cutting down on sodium is still an efficient and secure way to control blood pressure.
- Blood pressure reduction helps to lessen and ward against heart attacks and stroke.
- Hypertension is characterized by persistently high blood pressure.

Why are packaged foods added to sodium?

Sodium improves texture and appearance while enhancing taste and preserving freshness, and many products can achieve such effects at lower concentrations than are now being utilized. Many US food goods already have decreased salt content when offered in foreign nations, and this suggests that food producers release versions of well-known American items with less salt. Additionally, sodium levels in comparable US items vary significantly across brands and even within them, demonstrating that customers are willing to choose less salty goods.

Salt is an acquired taste, even though many food makers worry about the changed flavor of reduced sodium goods. According to some studies, consumers' taste receptors may become used to the flavor of lesser salt meals. According to several studies, when a popular product is offered in a reduced-sodium form, the average consumer replaces less than 20% of the salt that has been eliminated. This tendency implies that people are generally OK with items containing less salt over time.

Tips for a diet low in sodium

Low Sodium Diet

Your body only requires 1/4 teaspoon of salt each day. Although sodium occurs naturally in food, a significant amount is added when processed and prepared. Even if they don't taste salty, many meals contain a lot of sodium. Canned, processed, or ready-made foods may have significant salt levels. Additionally, many dishes provided in fast food establishments include salt.

Our bodies' fluid balance is regulated by sodium, which keeps blood volume and blood pressure stable. Consuming excessive amounts of salt may result in fluid retention and blood pressure elevation, which may cause swelling in the legs and feet and other health problems.

Consuming less than 2,000 mg daily of sodium is a popular target for lowering salt intake.

General instructions for salt reduction

- Cut down on your intake of salty foods and salt usage in cooking. Regular salt is superior to sea salt in no way.
- Opt for foods low in salt. There are several items with less salt or none at all. Low sodium is characterized as having a serving size of 140 mg of sodium on food labels.

- Always check the label since potassium is occasionally used to replace salt. Before utilizing such salt alternatives, consult your doctor if you are on a low-potassium diet.
- Use herbs, spices, lemon, garlic, ginger, vinegar, and pepper to season your cuisine. Take the salt shaker off the desk.
- Check food labels for salt content by reading the ingredient list. High-sodium foods contain 400 mg or more of salt per serving. Salt, brine, and other substances labeled sodium, such as monosodium glutamate, are examples of high-sodium food additives.
- Eat more meals prepared at home. Naturally, homemade meals have less salt than most fast and packaged mixes.
- Because softened water has additional salt, you shouldn't use it for drinking or cooking.
- Steer clear of drugs like Alka Seltzer and Bromo Seltzer that contain salt.
- Food composition books that list the amount of salt in food are available if you want further details. Amounts are listed on websites like www.calorieking.com.

Fish, Legumes, Poultry, Meat, Eggs, and nuts
  High-Sodium foods

- Meat, fish, or poultry that has been smoked, cured, salted, or canned, such as bacon, cold cuts,

ham, frankfurters, sausage, sardines, caviar, and anchovies.
- Frozen dishes like pizza and burritos that have been breaded
- Prepared meals in cans, including ravioli, spam, and chili
- Salted almonds
- Canned beans with salt added

Low-Sodium Alternatives

- all beef, lamb, pig, poultry, and fish, whether fresh or frozen
- eggs and egg alternatives
- salt-free peanut butter
- dried beans and peas (not canned)
- ish in a low-sodium can
- fish or poultry in water- or oil-packed, tinned form

Dairy Products
High-Sodium Foods

- buttermilk
- cheese spreads and sauces, both regular and processed
- cheese curds

Low-Sodium Alternatives

- ice milk, yogurt, milk, and ice cream
- low-sodium cheeses, including mozzarella, ricotta, and cream cheese

Bread, cereals, and grains
  High-Sodium Foods

- salted topping on bread and rolls
- self-rising flour, biscuit, pancake, and waffle mixes; quick bread;
- salted crackers, pizza, and croutons
- premade, processed potato, rice, pasta, and stuffing mixtures

Low-Sodium Alternatives

- unsalted topping on bread, bagels, and rolls
- most ready-to-eat cereals and muffins
- cook all types of rice and pasta without using salt
- corn and wheat tortillas, as well as low-sodium noodles
- low-sodium breadsticks and crackers
- unsalted pretzels, chips, and popcorn

Fruits and Veggies
High-Sodium Foods

- typical vegetable juices and canned goods
- sauerkraut, pickles, olives, and other pickled veggies
- vegetables cooked with a salted pig, bacon, or ham.
- premade mixes, such as frozen hash browns, tater tots, and potatoes au gratin or scalloped
- commercially available salsa, tomato sauces, and spaghetti

Low-Sodium Alternatives

- vegetables that are raw or frozen and aren't sauced
- canned veggies, sauces, and liquids with low-sodium
- instant mashed potatoes, frozen french fries, and fresh potatoes.
- Low-sodium tomato juice or v-8.
- most canned, frozen, and fresh fruit
- Dehydrated fruits

Soups
High-Sodium Foods

- commonly available canned and dried soup, broth, and bouillon
- ramen mix and cups of noodles

Low-Sodium Alternatives

- low-sodium broth, bouillon, and canned and dehydrated soups
- fresh soups cooked at home without salt

Desserts, sweets, and fats
Sodium-Rich Foods

- seasoning salt, soy sauce, and other sauces and marinades
- salad dressings in bottles, such as salad dressing with bacon pieces.
- margarine or butter with salt
- fast cake and pudding
- lots of ketchup and mustard

Low-Sodium Alternatives

- margarine, unsalted butter, or vinegar
- vegetable oils, sauces, and salad dressings low in salt
- mayonnaise
- all sweets are prepared without salt.

Final Thoughts

Reduce sodium consumption by looking at the Nutrition Facts label, using the% Daily Value (%DV) tool, and paying close attention to portions. Sodium is an essential component that the body needs in tiny quantities to keep bodily fluids in balance, keep muscles and nerves functioning properly, and prevent excessive perspiration. Reduce sodium intake by reading nutrition labels, making meals, buying fresh food, avoiding processed meats, observing vegetables, "rinsing" sodium with water, and eating fewer portions. Reducing salt consumption is an efficient and secure way to control blood pressure, save thousands of lives, and reduce the risk of heart disease and stroke. Salt is an acquired taste, and the average customer replaces less than 20% of the salt that has been eliminated when a popular product is presented in a reduced-sodium form.

Reduce salt intake, cut down on salty foods and salt usage in cooking, and opt for foods with less or no salt. Salt, brine, and other substances labeled sodium are examples of high-sodium food additives, so it is essential to avoid them. Low-Sodium

. . .

Alternatives include premade processed potato, rice, pasta, and stuffing mixtures, ready-to-eat cereals, and muffins, corn and wheat tortillas, low-sodium breadsticks and crackers, unsalted pretzels, chips, and popcorn, fruits and vegetables, soups, desserts, sweets, and fats, sodium-rich foods, seasonings, soy sauce, and marinades, and salad dressings.

The key features in this chapter

- Utilize the Nutrition Facts label as a tool to help you decide
- Be aware of Daily Value.
- Make use of the% Daily Value (%DV) tool.
- To determine how much sodium you ingest, consider the serving size and quantity you consume.
- To compare items accurately, utilize the Nutrition Facts label and remember to look at the serving size.
- Check for Nutritional Claims on the package. To rapidly find foods and drinks that could have less sodium, you can also look for nutritional claims on the packaging of such items.

4

SIGNS YOU'RE CONSUMING TOO MUCH SALT

How many salts do you need?

O ur body requires only a minimal quantity of sodium. Every day, we should consume roughly 1,500 milligrams of it; however, the typical American consumes approximately 3,400. High blood pressure, heart disease, and stroke may all be caused by excessive salt intake. However, how can you tell whether you're consuming too much salt?

You're Bloated

One of the most typical immediate symptoms of overeating salt is bloating, when your stomach feels inflated or tight. More fluid accumulates since it aids your body's ability to retain water. Foods may be rich in sodium without tasting salty, and Bagels, pizza, sandwiches, and canned soups are all potential sources of salt.

. . .

You have high blood pressure

Consuming too much salt is one of many possible causes of hypertension. Through your kidneys, your blood pressure changes, and they have a tougher time eliminating liquids you don't need when there is too much salt, and your blood pressure increases.

You're Puffy

An excessive amount of salt in your body may cause swelling. The most probable body areas to swell are your face, hands, feet, and ankles. Examine your intake of salt if you feel puffier than usual.

You're Thirsty

You may consume too much salt if you've been feeling thirsty recently. As a result, you start to feel dehydrated. As your body removes water from your cells, you can experience extreme thirst. The salt in your cells may be neutralized and refreshed by drinking water.

You have put on weight.

You might put on weight if you retain water. You may overeat salt if you've gained weight fast over a week or even a few days. Consider your recent food intake and attempt to make modifications to reduce the salt if you earn more than 2 pounds per day or 4 pounds per week.

You often use the bathroom.

More salt may result in more toilet visits. This can be the case because salt can produce extreme thirst, which might motivate you to consume more water. After that, you might use the bathroom more frequently than usual.

You're not getting good sleep

Before going to bed, overeating salt might disrupt your sleep. The symptoms might include insomnia, frequent nighttime awakenings, and morning fatigue.

You're Weak.

When your blood is overly salty, water gushes out of your cells to dilute the salt. The outcome? The possible onset of a weaker-than-normal feeling.

Your stomach gives you pain.

Your stomach will feel dehydrated if you consume too much salt, and you could get diarrhea or feel sick to your stomach. Examine what you've been eating over the last few days and find ways to reduce the salt if you have cramps or an upset stomach. Rehydrating your cells with lots of water will help you feel better.

Effects of too much salt over time

Overeating salt has long-term impacts and several short-term ones that should be avoided. A larger heart, frequent headaches, heart failure, high blood pressure, kidney illness, kidney stones, osteoporosis, stomach cancer, and stroke are all possible side effects.

How to reduce salt intake

Since nine out of ten Americans consume too much salt, there is a potential that you will as well.

To assist in controlling your levels:

- Select fresh meats over processed meats.
- When purchasing frozen veggies, choose "freshly frozen" and avoid those with sauces or seasonings already applied.
- Examine food labels and salt levels before purchasing.
- When picking spices and seasonings, choose ones whose labels don't mention salt.

If you go out to dine, you may request that the food be made without salt.

How to lower your salt intake

Food categories can vary in sodium content. Most of the sodium we consume comes from processed foods like those found in supermarkets and restaurants (not from the salt shaker). Foods that don't taste salty might yet contain a lot of sodium. Because they are consumed regularly, foods with just modest quantities of salt, like bread, may be significant sources of sodium.

Guidelines for Lowering Sodium Intake
In the supermarket

- Purchase unseasoned, unsalted, or sauce-free fresh, frozen, or canned veggies.
- When possible, choose packaged goods with labels labeled as "low sodium," "reduced sodium," or "no salt added."
- Examine the nutrition Facts labels on several goods to compare the salt content. Select the choices with the lowest salt content.
- The Food and Drug Administration's top guideline for a meal or main dish to be deemed "healthy" is 600 milligrams (mg) of salt each meal, so when purchasing prepared meals, opt for ones with less.
- It is essential to check the quantity of salt in each serving and the number of servings per container.
- Choose fresh chicken, fish, pig, and lean meat over processed meats like cured, salted, and smoked meats whenever feasible. Check whether saline or salt solution has been added to fresh foods; consider a different brand if it has.
- Inquire at your grocery store whether they have a list of low-sodium foods.
- To learn more about purchasing low-sodium goods, ask to talk to the trained dietitian at your neighborhood grocery shop. Ask your doctor for

a recommendation if your grocery store does not have a licensed dietician. A licensed dietician can provide insightful advice on controlling blood pressure and consuming less salt for your family.

At Home

- Use alternatives while cooking, such as garlic, lemon juice, salt-free seasonings, or spices, to replace or minimize the quantity of salt you use.
- When feasible, prepare grains, pasta, beans, and meats in their purest forms (dry and fresh).
- Increase the amount of produce you eat.
- Avoid using too many sauces, mixes, and quick foods, such as flavored rice and prepared spaghetti.

Dining Out

- Before placing an order, inquire about the nutrition facts and choose a meal with less salt.
- Request that your meal does not include any salt.
- Request fruit as a side dish or veggies without salt.
- Share a meal with a friend or member of your family.
- Reserve fast food and takeaway for special occasions.

Deciding on a heart-healthy diet

The easy, heart-healthy Dietary Approaches to Stop Hypertension (DASH) eating plan may help prevent or control high blood pressure. The DASH diet is abundant in fruits and vegetables, fiber, potassium, and low-fat dairy products while low in salt, cholesterol, and saturated fats.

The most prominent advantages come from adhering to the DASH diet plan and other healthy lifestyle adjustments like increasing physical activity.

Sodium: How to control your salt intake

How does sodium behave inside the body?

For the body to function effectively, sodium is required. Sodium contributes to:

- The harmony of your body's fluids

How nerves and muscles function?

The kidneys maintain the body's sodium equilibrium. The kidneys store salt when it is low, and the kidneys discharge some salt in urine when blood levels are high. When the kidneys cannot excrete enough salt, it accumulates in the blood. Because sodium draws and retains water, the volume of the blood rises. To pump blood, the heart must work harder, which raises artery pressure. This may increase the risk of renal, heart, and stroke disorders. Sodium affects some persons more than others, and they may thus more readily retain salt, which causes fluid retention and raises blood pressure.

. . .

What level of sodium is excessive?

Remember that less is preferable, particularly if you have salt sensitivity. Consult a dietician or your doctor if you need clarification on the recommended salt intake in your diet.

Which foods are sodium-rich?

Salt is a common ingredient in recipes; many diners season their meal before eating. Salt may also be found in condiments. For instance, 15 milliliters of soy sauce includes 1,000 mg of salt in one tablespoon. Sodium occurs naturally in several foods, including dairy, meat, seafood, and veggies. Although these meals don't contain a lot of salt, consuming them increases the sodium level of your body as a whole. For instance, 100 mg of sodium is present in 1 cup (237 milliliters) of low-fat milk.

How can I reduce my salt intake?

It would be beneficial for almost all Americans to consume less salt. Here are several strategies to make savings:

- Eat more fresh foods. Most fresh produce has naturally low salt content, and Additionally, fresh meat has less salt than ham, sausage, hot dogs, bacon, lunchmeat, and bacon products. Purchase fresh or frozen chicken or beef that hasn't had a sodium-containing solution injected into it. Check the label or inquire with your butcher.
- Select sodium-free items. When purchasing processed goods, look for those marked as low in

salt. Purchase plain, whole-grain rice and pasta rather than anything with flavors added.

- Eat at home. Many meals and snacks from restaurants are heavy in salt. The daily limit for one entrée may be reached or exceeded.
- Whenever you can, reduce the salt in recipes. You can omit salt from many recipes, including casseroles, soups, stews, and other substantial meals you prepare. Look for recipes that lower the risk of heart disease and high blood pressure.
- Use herbs, spices, and other flavorings instead of salt. Spice your dishes using fresh or dried herbs, spices, citrus juice, and zest.
- Limit your use of condiments. Sodium is an ingredient in soy sauce, salad dressings, sauces, dips, ketchup, mustard, and relish.

Verify the label.

You may be unable to identify meals rich in salt only by taste. For instance, a typical 4-inch (10-centimeter) oat bran bagel may not taste salty to you, but it has roughly 600 mg of sodium. Even a piece of whole-wheat bread has about 150 mg of sodium.

Which foods are thus high in salt, and how can you tell? Read the food labels. Most packaged and processed foods include a nutrition Facts label that consists of the salt content of each serving. Additionally, it states if salt or substances containing sodium are a component. Examples include:

- sodium mono glutamate (msg)
- flouring agent (also called sodium bicarbonate)
- baking soda
- phosphate dihydrate
- salt alginate
- citrate of sodium
- nitrite of sodium

Stay away from items containing 200 mg or more of salt per serving. Also, ensure you know how many servings are included in a container since the Nutrition Facts label contains that information.

Learn the lingo

Foods marked with low or light sodium are readily available in supermarkets, and you should only assume they are low in salt. For instance, even if a can of chicken noodle soup purports to have 25% less salt per cup, it still has a massive 524 mg. Only ordinary chicken noodle soup, which has more than 790 mg of sodium per cup, is lower in salt than this dish.

Following is a summary of typical sodium claims and what they imply:

- Free of salt or sodium. This product has a salt content per serving of less than 5 mg.
- Very little sodium. There are no more than 35 mg of salt per serving.
- Low in sodium. There are no more than 140 mg of salt per serving.

- Less or less salt. The product has at least 25% less salt than the ordinary form.
- Light or sodium light. At least 50% less sodium is present than in the original formulation.
- Food that has yet to have salt added. A food that ordinarily includes salt is processed without the addition of salt. Despite these labeling, specific components in some foods may still contain a lot of salt.

Use salt replacements carefully.

A salt replacement is created by substituting potassium, magnesium, or another mineral for part or all of the sodium. You can use too much of the alternative and consume too much sodium to obtain that familiar salty sensation.

For certain persons, the potassium in some salt replacements may be problematic. Too much potassium may be dangerous for those with renal issues or those who take medications, such as those prescribed to treat high blood pressure and congestive heart failure, which promote potassium retention.

Low and slowly, please

You might learn to appreciate less since your taste for salt is learned. Your taste senses will adapt as you progressively reduce your salt intake. For assistance with the adjustment, think about using salt-free spices. After a few weeks of salt restriction, you will get it; certain dishes could taste overly salty. Start by limiting your daily salt intake to no more than 1/4 teaspoon when eating and while cooking. After that, discard the saltshaker. Your liking for salt decreases as you use less, enabling you to appreciate the meal's flavor and heart-healthy advantages.

Ways to cut back on salt consumption

This shopping, cooking, and dining-out advice will help you consume less salt while still enjoying your meals. A pinch of salt beats a teaspoon regarding the amount of sodium you ingest and your health. Risk factors for chronic renal disease, heart disease, stroke, and high blood pressure: Salt excess is the leading cause of these health issues.

The Bill & Melinda Gates Foundation-funded Global Burden of Disease study found that excessive salt consumption is to blame for most diet-related deaths worldwide. The creator of NutritionFacts.org and a member of the US News Best Diets expert panel, Dr. Michael Greger, claims that excessive salt intake is the leading cause of death on Earth. The very worst thing we can do for our bodies is that.

The "great news" is that we have nearly complete control over this significant risk factor, according to Greger: "That's through lowering our consumption of processed foods and not adding salt at the table or when we're cooking."

Sodium levels: public health objectives

The American government has urged food manufacturers and restaurant owners to reduce salt content, and the objective is to avoid illnesses related to persistently ingesting too much salt. To make healthy adjustments in your diet, you don't need to wait for those slow, modest alterations to occur.

The Food and Drug Administration published voluntary salt reduction objectives for commercially processed, packaged, and prepared foods in October 2021. The FDA regulation covers 163 product categories and gives food makers, chain restaurants, and food service operators short-term salt reduction objectives.

According to Sharon Palmer, a registered dietitian from the Los Angeles area and author of books on plant-based nutrition and the Plant-Powered Dietitian blog, "We always understood that a lot of the salt was coming from packaged, processed, and prepared foods." "So, since it has such a big effect, the FDA appears to focus on it."

Daily Salt Recommendations

How much sodium should you aim for every day? The FDA wants to reduce American consumers' average daily salt consumption from around 3,400 milligrams to 3,000 milligrams, or about a teaspoon less, within two years. This revised sodium cap still exceeds the sodium guidelines provided by two distinct health organizations:

- Department of Agriculture. The USDA's Dietary Guidelines for Americans 2020–25 state that 2,300 mg of salt should be consumed daily by healthy individuals.
- United States Heart Association The American Heart Association advises individuals to consume no more than 2,300 milligrams of salt daily, with an optimal limit of no more than 1,500 milligrams, especially for those with high blood pressure.

Considering that some adults and children are already exhibiting negative impacts of poor diets, such as high blood pressure, dietary salt reduction is crucial for the whole family.

10 simple ways to reduce sodium

Discover 10 clever methods to reduce salt consumption without compromising taste. Sodium is hidden in many of our favorite foods, from bread to morning cereal.

As the American Heart Association advises, people should limit themselves to 1500 milligrams of salt daily. Many of us unknowingly consume a lot more than that because it hides in some surprising foods, including breakfast cereal, condiments, salad dressing, and canned goods, to name a few. Here's how to reduce your sodium intake and live a healthier life.

Put the salt shaker away.

Do not leave the salt shaker out on the table; if it is not easily accessible, you will be less likely to add salt while eating dinner, and when in doubt, the answer should be "no." You'd be astonished at how many of our eating habits are habitual.

Wash any canned veggies.

Salt has long been valued for its preservation properties, so many canned items are laden with it; thus, put your canned vegetables in a strainer and rinse the salt before cooking.

Purchase low-sodium goods.

Try these low-sodium dinners, and you won't miss the salt. It will taste a little different, but we hope you'll try it, as it can retrain your taste buds in only a few days, and you'll find that high-sodium foods taste like a salt lick. Low-sodium versions of everyday pantry staples like canned beans and chicken broth are now easily accessible.

Consume more fresh produce and fruits.

Switch your afternoon potato chip fix for crunchy apple or carrot sticks, or choose one of these fantastic salads instead of fries. Fries and chips may be created from potatoes, but they aren't the healthiest food choices, right? Regarding low- or no-salt foods, fruits and veggies are ideal.

Home cooking

On the other hand, you may regulate the salt content of your meals when you prepare them at home. Have fun with it. Try a new cuisine or favorite restaurant copycat recipe to keep your sodium in check. In restaurants, it might be challenging to determine the exact amount of salt in each dish.

Exercise restraint!

It is unrealistic to eliminate salt from your diet or cooking (and it's also not healthy), but you can be smart about it. Remember your portion sizes when dining out, and pack half your meal for later. The other option is to always ask for sauces and dressings on the side.

Change to fresh herbs or acids

Grow some on your windowsill and use them to enhance taste without resorting to salt. (Are you curious about how to preserve fresh herbs? I'll show you.) The acidity in vinegar and citrus fruits gives them a distinctive taste and doesn't hurt you nutritionally. Add a balsamic or red wine vinegar dash, or zest some lemons or limes for flavor.

Stock up on salt-free spice combinations in the cupboard.

In the spice aisle of your local supermarket, you'll discover a plethora of salt-free mixes. Some brands, like Mrs. Dash, don't include salt, while others provide salt-free or low-salt options. Instead of paying a firm to salt your food, you may do it to taste. Another option is to create your spice mixes and add as much salt as possible.

Check nutrition labels twice.

Since many major food producers, like Betty Crocker, Duncan Hines, and others, utilize their recipes, you can easily compare the components and nutrition of various brands of a packaged commodity, like a cake mix. Be mindful of portion sizes and seek the heart-healthy stamp of approval from the American Heart Association. Exciting news! According to the Food and Drug Administration, the food label is getting a makeover. The label will be easier to read and have more clearly stated serving sizes, calories, fat, and salt content.

List of foods low in sodium for a low-sodium diet

By skipping the saltshaker, you learn to enjoy your meals while consuming less sodium. Many people try to follow a low-sodium diet to support their health because frequent overconsumption of sodium is linked to many health problems, such as the development of high blood pressure and kidney damage.

Changing your diet to consume less sodium may be challenging because many packaged and prepared meals contain excessive salt. There are numerous less apparent sources of sodium in the diet, including chicken and turkey, pasta meals, bread, and sauces, and snacks like chips and pretzels are typical high-salt offenders. This section will assist you if you are beginning a low-sodium diet as you adjust to a new way of eating.

Talk to your doctor about the recommended limit if you have a medical condition like type 2 diabetes or chronic kidney disease since it may vary depending on your health and family history.

Dietary benefits of low sodium

We often add sodium to many of the meals we consume, frequently in the form of table salt. Because salt is necessary for many bodily processes, including nerve impulses, fluid balance, and muscle contraction, it is essential to include salt in your diet. Additionally, table salt may improve the taste of certain dishes and make meals more pleasurable.

But taking excessive amounts of salt may be harmful, resulting in high blood pressure and other health issues. On the other hand, maintaining a low-sodium diet is associated with several health advantages, such as:

- Suitable blood pressure
- Lower chance of cardiovascular disease development
- Better mental health
- Normal kidney (renal) function

According to a study, people who consume modest amounts of sodium may also notice immediate impacts like feeling less bloated or thirsty.

General recommendations for reducing sodium intake

You want to reduce salt consumption, but where do you begin? You'll be relieved to know that just minor adjustments to your diet will be necessary. Instead, even little adjustments and substitutions may make a considerable difference when lowering salt consumption. Here are some basic pointers to bear in mind for folks who are beginning their low-sodium diet:

- Don't season your food with salt before tasting it.
- Instead of salt, add extra herbs and spices to a meal to enhance the taste.
- Make your soup rather than buy canned varieties.

- Consider MSG, which tastes comparable to table salt but with about 60% less sodium.
- Make your salad dressing out of olive oil and vinegar to replace store-bought dressings.
- Before eating canned veggies and beans, rinse them with water or choose "no salt added" types.
- Pick fresh meat over highly processed choices, including deli meats, bacon, sausage, and jerky.
- Develop a practice of checking food labels to aid in selecting low-sodium items.
- When eating out, ask that your food not be salted.
- Eat less fast food since most of them have a lot of added salt.

A list of low-sodium foods to consume

With some knowledge, one may find meals with reduced salt content. Meals consumed in the most natural form are often lower in salt than foods that have undergone additional processing. Here are a few of the best low-sodium meals you should include in your diet to get you started. Remember that some of these foods can contain high levels of minerals that patients with chronic renal disease may need to avoid (like potassium). As a result, you should always get advice from your doctor before beginning any diet.

Veggies & Fruits

Fresh or freeze-dried fruits and vegetables are excellent, whether consumed with or without added salt or sodium. If they are not prepared with a salty sauce, frozen vegetables may be eaten while following a low-sodium diet. A low-sodium diet would benefit significantly from including plain frozen fruits and vegetables.

Salt is seldom used in canned fruit, and the best choice for canned veggies is the "no added salt" selection.

Good options for vegetables include:

- apples
- asparagus
- grapes
- mangoes
- mushrooms
- oranges
- potatoes
- strawberries
- spinach
- watermelon

Grains

Most grains may be significant components of a low-sodium diet as long as the foods you consume don't include salty ingredients (like soy sauce) or additional salt. Among the nutrient-dense options are:

- dark rice
- oats
- quinoa
- sorghum
- whole-wheat pasta

Proteins

Fortunately, many protein sources are inherently sodium-free. Protein serves various significant purposes in the body, and sodium and salt are often used to produce smoked, cured, and preserved meats. On the other hand, while eating a low-sodium diet, fresh cuts of beef, poultry, eggs, fish, and other proteins are acceptable.

When minimizing your salt intake, you may enjoy the following protein sources:

- dried legumes
- eggs
- fresh cuts of meat, hog, chicken, and seafood
- hummus
- nuts and peanuts without salt

Dairy

Magnesium, potassium, and calcium, minerals that maintain good blood pressure, are abundant in many dairy products. However, certain dairy products, including several kinds of cheese, may also be high in salt. Fortunately, several delectable dairy products are high in nutrients and low in salt, such as:

- butter without salt
- kefir
- milk
- plain half-and-half
- yogurtSwiss chard

Fat

A balanced diet should include healthy fats. A few choices may also be rich in antioxidants and essential vitamins, such as vitamin E. A low-sodium diet is OK with the following healthy fat sources:

- avocados
- avocado oil
- chia, flax, and hempseed seeds
- unsalted nuts, including almonds, cashews, pistachios, and peanuts, as well as their nut butter.
- oily fish, including sardines, tuna, and salmon
- olive oil

Foods with high sodium content to avoid

It's easy to find low-sodium items that can be included in a diet. Fresh fruit and roasted chicken breast seasoned with fresh herbs are just two mouthwatering dishes that those following a low-sodium diet may savor.

However, since they are notoriously high in sodium, certain foods should be on your "once-in-a-while foods" list if you are on a low-sodium diet. Most salt consumed in the US comes from packaged and restaurant cuisine. When beginning your low-sodium journey, eating more meals at home and choosing healthier food might be a fantastic start. While it comes to certain foods, there are several that are often high in sodium and are thus advisable to restrict when following a low-sodium diet, such as:

- cans of pasta
- cheese, cheddar
- french bread
- ham
- hotdogs
- pasta sauce in jars
- pickles
- pretzels
- salted almonds
- sauce soy
- teriyaki condiment
- vegetable liqueur

To sum up, you don't have to survive on bland chicken breast and dry vegetables if you eat a low-sodium diet. Maintaining a lower-sodium diet while enjoying your favorite meals may be accomplished by having fresh fruit, unsalted almonds, yogurt, and pasta. Without adding even a grain of salt, herbs and spices like garlic, turmeric, or freshly cracked pepper will satisfy your taste buds. Eat low-sodium meals all day, starting with Veggie & Hummus Sandwiches for lunch and Chicken Cutlets with Sun-Dried Tomato Cream Sauce for dinner. You can maintain a healthy salt consumption while still feeling content and fed.

4 myths that make you consume more salt than you realize

Discover the typical sodium myths that encourage Americans to consume excessive amounts of the mineral, which may have adverse health effects.

- There is a sodium issue in America. For many years, experts have expressed concern about excessive salt consumption in the typical American diet and have issued health-related warnings.
- The issue is that many Americans need to be made aware of what they are doing or where the salt in their diet truly comes from.
- The risk of health issues, including high blood pressure, heart disease, and stroke, rises when sodium consumption is at this level.
- You're trying to limit your salt intake, and it's critical to understand where your salt consumption comes from. Tip: It may not be potato chips.

Misconceptions regarding sodium intake

MYTH #1: Salting your meal at the table results in high sodium consumption.

In truth, just a tiny fraction of the sodium consumed by the typical American comes from table salt. In reality, processed, packaged food (such as frozen pizza or boxed mac and cheese) and restaurant meals account for most of our daily salt consumption.

MYTH #2: Consuming salty snacks leads to high sodium consumption.

When they think of salt, most people associate salt with salty foods like nuts, chips, and pretzels. However, according to the 2015-2020 Dietary Guidelines for Americans, salty snacks only comprise a minor portion of the typical American diet's sodium consumption. Although it is not trivial, it's crucial to understand where most of the salt comes from if you are serious about reducing your sodium consumption.

Surprisingly, bread (!), pizza, deli meat, and soup are among the highest sources of salt in the typical American diet. Remember that many items are considered restaurant cuisine or highly processed foods. Adding sodium to food may improve taste and extend shelf life.

MYTH #3: By choosing "healthy" selections, you can stay away from high-sodium restaurant meals

Even restaurant salads may contain a shocking amount of salt. Even more, salt may be found in certain salads at chain restaurants than in a bacon cheeseburger. Salad dressing, toppings like croutons, and meats like cold cuts or fried chicken might conceal salt sources. Check the nutritional information on a chain restaurant's website before going, or ask your waiter if you're worried about the amount of salt in the food.

MYTH #4: Choosing items with decreased salt content is the greatest approach to avoid consuming too much sodium.

Many individuals may switch to reduced-sodium items to consume less salt. For instance, you may purchase canned beans with no added salt, chicken broth with less sodium, low-salt almonds, and canned soup with less sodium.

Items with less salt might help you consume less overall. However, consuming fewer processed meals is an even more effective strategy to minimize salt consumption. Consuming meals created with fresh, complete foods can help you consume less salt. For instance, homemade soup often has less salt than canned soup with reduced sodium.

The implications of consuming too much sodium

If you need help understanding the exact sources of salt in your diet, it might be challenging to reduce your intake. Recording your daily sodium consumption in a food diary could help you acquire a more accurate diet picture. Consult a qualified nutritionist for assistance in lowering your salt consumption.

Final Thoughts

Excessive salt intake can lead to bloating, swelling, dehydration, high blood pressure, heart disease, and stroke. Too much salt can have long-term and short-term health effects, so it is essential to reduce it.

The most important details are to purchase unseasoned, unsalted, or sauce-free fresh, frozen, or canned veggies, choose packaged goods with labels labeled as "low sodium," "reduced sodium," or "no salt added," and use alternatives while cooking. Sodium is essential for the body to function effectively and is found in many foods, such as prepared meals, condiments, dairy, meat, seafood, and veggies. It can also cause fluid retention and raised blood pressure.

Reduce salt intake by eating more fresh foods, selecting sodium-free items, taking salt out of recipes, using herbs, spices, and other flavorings instead of salt, and limiting condiments. Cut back on salt intake by limiting daily salt intake to no more than 1/4 teaspoon, using salt-free spices, and using salt replacements carefully. Excessive salt intake is the leading cause of death on Earth, but we can reduce it through reduced consumption of processed foods and not adding salt to the table or when cooking. Reduce sodium intake and live healthier by washing canned vegetables, purchasing low-sodium goods, and putting the salt shaker away. Consume more fresh produce and fruits, exercise restraint, and use salt-free spice combinations.

Check nutrition labels twice and seek the heart-healthy stamp of approval. Low sodium intake can help people live healthier lives but can also lead to health issues such as high blood pressure and kidney damage. Low-sodium diets should include simple adjustments and substitutions to reduce salt consumption, such as not seasoning food before tasting it, making soup with herbs and spices, making salad dressing with olive oil and vinegar, and picking fresh meat over highly processed. Low-sodium diets should include protein sources such as fresh cuts of meat, eggs, dairy, dried legumes, nuts, nuts, and hummus, as well as healthy fats such as olive oil, avocado oil, avocados, and other fats. Avoid foods with high sodium content to avoid.

Reduce salt consumption by eating low-sodium meals, adding herbs and spices, and understanding where it comes from. Consuming salty snacks leads to high sodium consumption, but bread, pizza, deli meat, and soup are among the highest sources of salt in the typical American diet. Choosing reduced-sodium items and consuming fewer processed meals can help reduce salt consumption.

The key features in this chapter

- Consult a dietician or your doctor if you need clarification on the recommended salt intake in your diet.
- Use salt replacements carefully.
- Keeping salt levels in control may be accomplished by adhering to a low-sodium diet or eating plan.
- Greger believes that a low-salt diet might improve salt sensitivity.
- Stock up on salt-free spice combinations in the cupboard.
- Another option is to create your spice mixes and add as much salt as possible.
- Check nutrition labels twice.
- Many protein sources are inherently sodium-free.
- Consuming salty snacks leads to high sodium consumption.

Dear Reader,

As independent authors, it's often difficult to gather reviews compared with much bigger publishers.

Therefore, please leave a review on the platform where you bought this book.

KINDLE:

<u>LEAVE A REVIEW HERE < click here ></u>

Many thanks,

Author Team

5

DIETS LOW IN SODIUM: ADVANTAGES, FOOD RECOMMENDATIONS, RISKS, AND MORE

T he phrase "low-sodium diet" refers to a diet with restricted salt consumption. Expert panels' definitions of "low sodium" vary and may alter if a person has a particular illness, such as chronic renal disease. The optimal limit of daily salt intake is 1,500 mg for most people, particularly those with high blood pressure.

Even though salt is required for proper bodily function, it may be necessary to limit intake under some circumstances. For instance, a low-sodium diet is often recommended for those with certain medical conditions, including heart disease, hypertension, and renal illness. This section discusses the advantages, hazards, and items to consume and avoid and why some individuals need to follow a low-sodium diet.

A low-sodium diet: what is it?

Your kidneys closely control the amount of this mineral in your body since it is essential to life and depends on physiological fluids' osmolarity (concentration). Most things you consume include sodium.

However, meals like fruits, vegetables, and poultry have far lower quantities.

Fresh fruit and other plant-based foods often contain less salt than animal-based meals like meat and dairy. Because salt is added during processing to enhance flavor, processed and packaged goods like chips, frozen dinners, and fast food tend to have the greatest sodium.

Adding salt to food during cooking and seasoning before eating significantly contributes to sodium consumption. High-sodium meals and drinks are restricted to a low-sodium diet. Healthcare professionals often advise these diets to manage ailments like high blood pressure or heart disease.

Although there are exceptions, the recommended daily salt consumption is less than 2-3 grams (2,000–3,000 mg) which is the amount in one teaspoon of salt. To maintain your salt consumption below the recommended range when on a low-sodium diet, items rich in sodium must be restricted or altogether avoided.

How Are low-sodium diets recommended?

One of the most popular diets in hospital settings is low in salt. A study shows sodium restriction may help regulate or improve several medical disorders.

· · ·

Kidney Disease

Kidney disease adversely affects kidney function, including chronic renal disease (CKD) and kidney failure. When your kidneys are damaged, they can't correctly rid your body of extra fluid or salt.

Your blood pressure increases if salt and fluid levels become too high, which might further harm your kidneys' already damaged tissues. The National Kidney Foundation advises all individuals with CKD to limit their daily salt consumption to less than 2 grams (2,000 mg). In CKD patients, modest sodium restriction effectively lowered blood pressure and protein in the urine, according to a review of 11 trials (a marker of kidney damage).

High Blood Pressure

Heart disease and stroke are two illnesses for which high blood pressure raises the risk. In a recent research of 766 individuals, for instance, it was shown that those with the most significant amounts of salt excretion in the urine also had the highest blood pressure levels.

Numerous studies have shown that reducing salt may help patients with high blood pressure lower it. Salt restriction decreased blood pressure in adults, with the biggest effects shown in individuals with high blood pressure, according to a study of six research involving more than 3,000 participants.

There is a considerable range in the salt sensitivity of persons with high blood pressure. Specific populations, such as African Americans, appear more affected by high-salt diets. However, low-sodium diets are often suggested as a non-pharmacological therapy for anybody with high blood pressure.

. . .

Heart Disease

Diets low in salt are often advised for those with cardiac issues, such as heart failure. Kidney function deteriorates when your heart is impaired, which may cause salt and water retention.

Consuming too much salt may result in fluid overload and serious problems, including shortness of breath in persons with heart failure.

Regulating bodies advise that people with mild heart failure should limit their daily salt intake to 3,000 mg, while those with moderate to severe heart failure should limit it to no more than 2,000 mg. While several researchers have shown the value of low-sodium diets for people with heart failure, other studies have found that non-restrictive diets provide superior results. For instance, a research of 833 heart failure patients revealed that unrestricted-sodium diets with 2,500 mg or more of sodium per day were substantially related to a lower risk of mortality or hospitalization than restricted-sodium diets with less than 2,500 mg per day.

Dietary benefits of low sodium

A low-sodium diet may be advantageous to health in several ways.

Could lower blood pressure

- A low-sodium diet, as previously mentioned, may aid in lowering blood pressure.
- According to studies, switching to a low-sodium diet may lower blood pressure, particularly in

those with excessive levels. These improvements can be subtle but essential.

- Researchers found that participants in 34 studies with high and normal blood pressure experienced significant drops in their blood pressure when their salt intake was moderately reduced for four or more weeks.

The average decrease in systolic and diastolic blood pressure in patients with high blood pressure was 5.39 mmHg and 2.82 mmHg, respectively. In contrast, those with normal levels dropped 1.00 mmHg in diastolic blood pressure and 2.42 mmHg in systolic blood pressure (the bottom number of a reading).

Might Reduce Cancer Risk

High salt intake has been related to many malignancies, including stomach cancer. According to a study of 76 research involving more than 6,300,000 persons, the risk of stomach cancer rose by 12% for every five grams of dietary salt consumed daily from processed foods with high salt content.

According to research, eating a lot of salt may harm the mucosal lining of your stomach, cause inflammation, and promote the development of H. Pylori bacteria, which may increase your chance of developing stomach cancer. Conversely, a diet heavy in fresh produce and low in processed foods with high salt levels is linked to a decreased risk of stomach cancer.

Might enhance dietary quality

Many unhealthy foods include a lot of salt. Fast food, packaged goods, and frozen meals are rich in calories and harmful fats and are salt-laden.

Obesity, diabetes, and heart disease have all been related to the frequent use of these foods. These high-salt items are forbidden on a low-sodium diet, which may enhance the nutritional quality of your diet.

Foods to Avoid

On a low-sodium diet, the following items should be avoided because they are rich in sodium:

- Fast food items include burgers, fries, chicken fingers, and pizza.
- Salty snack items include salty chips, pretzels, almonds, and crackers.
- Freeze-dried meals, such as frozen pizza and beef dishes.
- Meats such as lunch, hot dogs, and bacon have been processed.
- Canned and salted foods like vegetables, pasta, pork, and fish.
- Salty Soups: packaged and canned soups.
- Dairy and cheese: cheese, cheese sauce, cheese spreads, cottage cheese, buttermilk, and salted butter.
- Salted rolls, bagels, croutons, and crackers are examples of baked foods high in sodium.
- Baking mixes: waffle, pancake, or cake mixes high in salt.

- Boxed meals include macaroni and cheese, spaghetti, and rice dishes.
- Side dishes high in sodium: rice pilaf, hash browns, packaged potatoes au gratin, and stuffing.
- Gravy, soy, canned tomato, salsa, and salad dressing are sauces and condiments.
- Pickled vegetables, such as sauerkraut, pickles, and olives.
- Some alcoholic beverages with salt, regular vegetable juice, juice mixes, etc.
- Seasonings include salt and salt mixtures.

Although certain foods, such as vegetables and unprocessed meats, naturally contain trace salt levels, these amounts pale compared to the sodium added to meals prepared for sale. Restricting salty snacks, fast food, and prepared meals is the greatest method to avoid high-sodium foods.

Enjoyable low-sodium foods

If you're trying to reduce the amount of sodium in your diet, choosing foods with low sodium content or little added salt is essential. When following a low-sodium diet, it is okay to consume the following foods:

- Vegetables, fresh and frozen (no sauces): greens, broccoli, cauliflower, peppers, etc.
- Fruits: Berries, apples, bananas, pears, etc.; fresh, frozen, or dried.

- Grains and legumes: whole wheat pasta, brown rice, farro, and dried beans.
- Potatoes, sweet potatoes, butternut squash, and parsnips are starchy vegetables.
- Fresh or frozen meat and poultry, including beef, hog, chicken, and turkey.
- Frozen or fresh fish, cod, sea bass, and tuna.
- Eggs: both whole and white eggs.
- Olive oil, avocados, and avocado oil are good fats.
- Low-sodium canned or homemade soups are available.
- Milk, yogurt, unsalted butter, and low-sodium cheeses are examples of dairy products.
- Whole-wheat bread, low-sodium tortillas, and unsalted crackers are examples of bread and baked products.
- Unsalted nuts and seeds include peanuts, almonds, and pumpkin seeds.
- Unsalted pretzels, unsalted popcorn, and unsalted tortilla chips are low-sodium snacks.
- Low-sodium condiments include vinegar, mayonnaise, salad dressing, and sauces.
- Tea, coffee, low-sodium vegetable juice, and water are all examples of low-sodium drinks.
- Low-sodium seasonings include garlic powder, no-salt mixes, herbs, and spices.

Potential Risks

Major health organizations advise individuals to take no more than 2,300 mg of salt daily, and higher-risk populations, such as African Americans and older persons, to consume no more than 1,500 mg (20). It was evident that high-salt diets raise the risk of stomach cancer and that a reduced-sodium diet may lower blood pressure in those with excessive levels. Still, the evidence for additional advantages of cutting down on this crucial mineral is mixed.

For instance, even though sodium restriction is often used to treat heart failure, some research has shown that doing so may harm patient health. According to research including 833 heart failure patients, eating less salt—less than 2,500 mg daily—was linked with a considerably greater mortality risk or hospitalization than eating more sodium than usual.

Similar findings have been seen in other investigations.

Furthermore, studies have shown that ingesting insufficient salt might harm heart health. Analysis of 23 studies found that extremes in salt intake were associated with an elevated threat of cardiovascular disease and mortality overall. Inadequate salt consumption has also been connected to several other harmful health outcomes.

Consuming insufficient salt may result in hyponatremia, insulin resistance, and elevated cholesterol and triglycerides (too little sodium in the blood). While it's always a good idea to steer clear of high-sodium, unhealthy foods like fast food, most healthy people don't need to restrict their salt intake when they eat a balanced diet rich in whole foods.

Tips for a low-sodium diet

It might be challenging to season dishes and make meals tasty if you follow a low-sodium diet. However, there are a lot of quick methods to add flavor to meals without adding salt.

Here are some pointers for prepping and preparing low-sodium meals:

- You may use lemon juice for salt if you want.
- Use fresh herbs in place of salt while cooking.
- Try out some different spices.
- Create a vibrant, zesty salad dressing using olive oil and citrus juices.
- Snack on unsalted nuts that have been seasoned with various spices.
- Prepare a homemade soup with ginger and garlic flavoring.
- Include extra fresh fruit and vegetables in your meals and snacks.
- Make your hummus at home using dried chickpeas and add garlic and herbs for taste.
- Combine olive oil, garlic, vinegar, honey, and ginger to make a low-sodium marinade.

Increase your home cooking

According to a study, foods consumed outside the house are the primary source of salt consumption. According to a survey of 450 people from various regions, 70.9% of the total salt consumed was in dishes from restaurants and other commercial establishments. One of the ideal ways to reduce the amount of salt in your diet is to cook your meals at home, where you have more control over what goes into them.

Along with lowering salt consumption, eating more meals at home may aid in weight loss.

According to research involving more than 11,000 individuals, people who made more meals at home had lower body fat and higher overall diet quality than those who ate less food prepared at home.

Chronic renal disease, high blood pressure, and food quality, in general, may all be helped by low-salt diets. They could also lower the risk of stomach cancer. However, too little salt may harm health, and most individuals don't need to follow this diet. If you consume a low-sodium diet, choose fresh meals and avoid salty ones. Another excellent strategy to manage your salt consumption and adhere to your doctor's advice is to cook more meals at home.

Guidelines for a low-salt diet

It just takes a little effort and some instruction from reliable sources to learn how to reduce your salt intake. Use the following advice to get acquainted with the finest low-sodium meals and monitor your daily intake:

Track your intake

Utilizing a nutrition tracking app, start by monitoring your current salt consumption.

This is a simple approach to determining where the bulk of the sodium in your diet originates, where to start making healthy substitutions, and how to ensure you are following the suggested standards and eating a low-sodium diet.

There are various methods to keep track of your consumption. You may use a food diary or fitness software like the Trifecta App or determine how many calories you need daily.

Create a Meal Plan

Another fantastic strategy to take charge of your nutrition is to plan part or all of your meals. This is especially beneficial since you'll always know what you're eating. To be successful, you don't need detailed instructions or expensive supplies. Instead, start with easy meal suggestions and see what suits you. Make food selections and a weekly menu plan for your heart-healthy meals with our free menu planning template.

Numerous diets, including the paleo, keto, vegan, whole foods, and flexitarian ones, may be adapted to be low in sodium as long as the emphasis is placed on eating fresh, whole foods and the amount of salt used in cooking is kept to a minimum.

When organizing your meals for a low-salt diet, keep the following in mind:

- Decide to cook a few meals at home each week to increase your home-cooked meals gradually.
- Use less prepared sauces, mixes, "instant" foods, and prepared sides from the shop.

- Consider buying fresh products like meat, poultry, fruits and vegetables, and whole grains.
- Choose fresh vegetables over canned or frozen ones, or search for canned foods with minimal sodium or salt added.
- Rinse canned goods like beans to get rid of extra salt.
- Invest in unsalted or no-salt snacks like almonds or vegetable sticks.
- Drinks also include salt; stick to water instead of anything else.

Learn to have a food plan for your lunches and prepare nutritious meals at home to take control of the situation.

Eat more organic, fresh foods.

Use the following list of naturally low-sodium foods to guide your shopping list!

Remember that the freshest produce, including fruits and vegetables, raw, unprocessed meats, uncooked whole grains, and anything else, is likely low in salt. If the product is packed, additional salt is more likely.

Additionally, meals rich in potassium have an asterisk next to them since potassium is known to help offset some of the negative consequences of consuming large amounts of salt. Most fresh fruits and vegetables are usually strong sources of potassium and other healthy minerals, making them a great option.

Although certain foods may be heavier in salt than others, remember that your diet is the sum of everything you consume in a day. As a result, by planning your meals carefully, you can balance out your daily consumption.

. . .

Fruits and Vegetables

All fruits are low in sodium as long as they are fresh and unprocessed.

- Bananas*
- Melons*
- Oranges* & Citrus
- Apples
- Grapes
- Berries (strawberries, blueberries, etc.)
- Kiwi
- Papaya
- Guava

All Fresh and frozen unsalted vegetables

- No-salt-added or low-sodium canned vegetables or tomatoes
- Leafy Greens*
- Potatoes
- Tomatoes
- Zucchini
- Butternut Squash
- Spaghetti Squash
- Spinach
- Kale
- Green Beans
- Cruciferous Vegetables (broccoli, cauliflower, brussel sprouts, etc.)

- Whole Grains
- Beans and Legumes*
- Brown or Wild Rice
- Quinoa
- Barley
- CousCous
- Whole-wheat or whole-grain pasta
- Oats or shredded wheat
- Unsalted Popcorn
- Low-Sodium Chips and Pretzels
- Whole-Grain Bread, bagels, English muffins, tortillas, and crackers
- Homemade waffles & pancakes with no salt
- Rice Noodles/No-salt noodles
- Any processed grains or cereals with more than 180 mg sodium per serving
- If Canned, choose low-sodium or no-sodium:
- Kidney Beans
- Pinto Beans
- Black Beans
- Lima Beans
- Black-Eyed Peas
- Garbanzo Beans (chickpeas)
- Split Peas
- Lentils
- Nuts & Seeds (Unsalted)

Unseasoned proteins & seafood

- All seeds and nuts, as long as they are unsalted:
- Almonds

- Peanuts
- Pumpkin Seeds
- Pine Nuts
- Sunflower Seeds
- Chia Seeds
- Flax Seeds
- All proteins, as long as they are unseasoned, no marinades, etc.:
- Eggs
- Salmon*
- Chicken (breast, thigh, whole, ground)
- Turkey
- Beef (ground, steak, etc.)
- Pork
- Lamb & Veal
- Fresh or frozen fish and seafood
- Low-Sodium canned tuna

Dairy Products

- Fats, Oils & Vinegar
- Low fat-milk* and milk products
- Yogurt (greek)
- Low-Sodium Cheese
- Soymilk
- All oils and all vinegars are considered low-sodium:
- Grapeseed Oil
- Flaxseed Oil
- Nut Oils (walnut, almond, sunflower, etc.)
- Apple Cider Vinegar

* Foods rich in potassium

High-sodium foods to avoid

The bulk of salt consumption occurs when people dine at restaurants, fast food restaurants, or consume a lot of packaged and prepared goods, such as:

- Sauces, including ketchup, teriyaki, BBQ, marinara, soy sauce, and salad dressings.
- Soups
- Foods in cans
- Salty Snacks: As a general rule, avoid eating anything that has salt visible on it. Salted crackers, pretzels, chips, almonds, etc.
- Bagels, tortillas, bread, and biscuits
- Processed meats: These meats, such as bacon, sausage, lunch, hot dogs, and the like, are often preserved by curing or high salt content.
- Pizza
- Frozen foods and meals, such as frozen processed meats, pizza, and dishes
- Cottage cheese and cheese
- Pickled vegetables and meals
- Salted seeds and nuts
- Butter with salt
- Salt-seasoned condiments

Additionally, the following foods naturally have more sodium:

- clams
- crab thighs

- beets

Read Food Labels

Always read the nutrition facts label on packaged foods to see how much salt is in them before consuming them. Anything with less than 5% of the recommended daily salt intake is generally considered "low," while anything with more than 20% is usually considered "high." Next time you go grocery shopping, use this simple chart to grasp fundamental salt claims and make product selections:

Label Claim Meaning

Salt/sodium-free

Less than 5 mg of sodium per serving

Very low sodium

35 mg of sodium or less per serving

Low Sodium

140 mg of sodium or less per serving

Reduced Sodium

At least 25% less sodium than the original product

Light in Sodium or Lightly Salted

At least 50% less sodium than the original product

No-Salt-Added or Unsalted

No salt is added during processing – but these products may not be salt/sodium-free

Reduce salt when dining out or cooking at home more

Ask your waitress to leave off the salt if you can, whether dining at a restaurant or getting anything cooked away from home. You may also choose foods with less complex components instead of often-used high-sodium elements like sauces, breading, and cheese. Try grilled chicken breast, for instance, instead of chicken parmesan. If you want to know the restaurant's nutrition information in advance, you may either check their website or ask the staff. This lets you accurately determine how much salt is in your chosen dish.

Use different seasonings

Without constantly using salt, flavoring your cuisine to the hilt is feasible. Avoiding salt but still packing flavor is possible using herbs, spices, and condiments like vinegar. As a bonus, fresh and dried herbs and spices will provide modest quantities of beneficial minerals and phytonutrients.

Here are some excellent sodium-free salt substitutes:

- herbs, both fresh and dried
- juice and zest of citrus
- citrus pepper
- paprika
- garlic
- ginger
- powdered onion
- vinegar like balsamic or apple cider
- chili flakes
- cumin
- coriander
- pepper
- any seasoning mixture devoid of salt

Sample Diet Menu

Here is an example of a straightforward, healthful, low-sodium diet that involves minimal food preparation and won't break the wallet to assist you in getting started.

- 1500 calories per day
- 566 mg of sodium overall per day
- 3,556 mg of potassium daily.

Breakfast

Nutrition

- 1/2 cup oatmeal cooked with 1/2 cup skim milk
- 1 tsp honey
- 1 banana

327 calories

128 mg sodium

1014 mg potassium

Lunch

Nutrition

- 4 oz grilled chicken breast
- 2 cups of leafy greens
- 1/8 cup shredded carrots
- 1/8 cup cherry tomatoes
- 1/4 cup dried apricots

- 1/3 avocado
- 1 tbsp fresh lemon juice
- 1 tbsp olive oil
- Cracked pepper

513 calories

213 mg sodium

1569 mg potassium

Dinner

Nutrition

- 4 oz salmon, lightly seasoned
- 1/2 cup cooked brown rice
- 1 cup steamed broccoli seasoned with 1/2 tsp lemon pepper

401 calories

222 mg sodium

590 mg potassium

Snack

Nutrition

- 1 Apple
- 1/4 cup unsalted almonds
- 1 piece dark chocolate

273 calories

3 mg sodium

383 mg potassium

Not interested in cooking your meals or struggling to keep your salt consumption in check? You can put your sodium-controlled diet on autopilot by selecting a reputable meal delivery service that offers pre-cooked meats, grains, and vegetables with few spices.

Final Thoughts

Low-sodium diets are recommended for specific medical conditions, such as heart diseases, hypertension, and renal illness, and can help regulate or improve several medical disorders. Kidney and heart disease are two illnesses for which high blood pressure is linked to a high-sodium diet. Low-sodium diets are suggested as a non-pharmacological therapy for those with high blood pressure. Low-sodium diets can help lower blood pressure, reduce cancer risk, and improve dietary quality. Restricting salty snacks, fast food, and prepared meals is the best way to avoid high-sodium foods.

Low-sodium foods include vegetables, fruits, grains, legumes, meat and poultry, eggs, canned or homemade soups, dairy products, bread and baked products, unsalted nuts and seeds, snacks, condiments, tea, coffee, low-sodium vegetable juice, and water. Consuming insufficient salt can lead to hyponatremia, insulin resistance, and elevated cholesterol and triglycerides, but most healthy individuals don't need to limit their salt intake.

Increase home cooking to reduce salt consumption and adhere to the doctor's advice. Plan a low-salt diet by cooking a few meals at home each week, paying attention to fresh products, choosing fresh vegetables over canned or frozen ones, investing in unsalted or no-salt snacks, and eating more organic, fresh foods.

High-sodium foods to avoid are sauces, soups, snacks, processed meats, frozen foods, pickled vegetables, salted seeds and nuts, butter with salt, and salt-seasoned condiments. Choose foods with less complex components instead of high-sodium elements, and use herbs, spices, and condiments to avoid salt.

The key features in this chapter

- According to studies, switching to a low-sodium diet may lower blood pressure, particularly in those with excessive levels.
- Restricting salty snacks, fast food, and prepared meals is the greatest method to avoid high-sodium foods.
- When following a low-sodium diet, it is okay to consume the following foods: • Vegetables, fresh and frozen (no sauces): greens, broccoli, cauliflower, peppers, etc.
- If you want to know the restaurant's nutrition information in advance, you may either check their website or ask the staff.
- Use different seasonings. Without constantly using salt, flavoring your cuisine to the hilt is feasible.

6

YOUR SHOPPING LIST FOR HEART-HEALTHY FOODS

P roper heart-healthy items in your kitchen are the first step towards healthy eating, and they assist in lowering cholesterol and controlling blood pressure. You can print out this list and bring it to the grocery store if you still need to decide what to purchase.

Essentials for the refrigerator

Fresh produce is an excellent source of vitamins, minerals, and other nutrients. They also include fiber, which helps to decrease cholesterol and promotes heart health. When you want to eat, take them out first. Remember that you need 5 cups of fruits and vegetables daily.

- apples
- berries
- bell peppers
- broccoli
- cauliflower
- celery

- deep green leaves
- eggplant
- grapes
- kale
- oranges
- pears
- squash
- tomatoes
- zucchini

Dairy and Dairy Substitutes: Dairy is a fantastic calcium source. Omit the cream and go for low- or nonfat choices instead.

- Light or nonfat cream cheese
- Low-fat or nonfat cheese
- Milk, 1% or skim
- Nonfat or 1% cottage cheese or ricotta cheese
- Nonfat or 1% yogurt
- Nonfat creamers
- Nonfat or low-fat buttermilk
- Nonfat sour cream

You could also choose soy, almond, and other non-dairy options. To prevent additional sugar, consider the unsweetened varieties of these beverages while shopping. The American Heart Association recommends two meals of fish per week for those who consume meat, poultry, fish, and meat substitutes. Consume more tofu and other heart-healthy soy proteins, and avoid consuming too much fatty meat.

- Beef, lean cuts, including lean sirloin or ground round
- Ground chicken or turkey
- Omega-3-rich fish, such as herring, mackerel, salmon, trout, and tuna
- Skinless, boneless chicken or turkey breasts and tenders
- Seitan
- Tempeh
- Tofu
- Trimmed-of-fat pork tenderloin

Foods that are frozen: When your favorite fruits and vegetables are out of season, consider frozen foods to make wholesome desserts, sides, and snacks.

- Fruits without sugary additives (for example, frozen blueberries, raspberries, and strawberries)
- Soybeans (edamame)
- Vegetables and vegetable mixtures devoid of salt, sauce, or gravy pantry necessities

Beans, whole grains, soups, and sauces include fiber that may help decrease cholesterol.

- Barley
- Beans, canned, reduced-sodium: various beans, including pinto, navy, garbanzo, and kidney beans.

- Broth, chicken, meat, or vegetables with low sodium
- Cornmeal
- Dried beans: Pick your preferred beans.
- Grains including quinoa, bulgur, millet, couscous, polenta, and wheat berries
- Ground or whole flaxseed
- Irish, rolled, or steel-cut oats
- Low-fat or fat-free pasta sauce
- Low-sodium soups with cream of mushroom that are 98% fat-free.
- Nonfat or vegetarian refried beans
- Oat bran
- Rice: wild, brown, and basmati
- Tomahawk sauce
- Wheat flour
- Whole-grain cereals (Note: Opt for cereals with 5 grams or more of less than 8 grams of sugar and dietary fiber per serving.)
- Whole or diced tomatoes with low sodium
- Whole wheat flour
- Whole wheat, spelled, or kamut pasta (Note: These whole-grain pastas come in a bowtie, fettuccini, lasagna, spaghetti, fusilli, spiral, elbow macaroni, and ravioli varieties.)

Sauces and condiments with a lot of salt should be avoided. Even tiny sums quickly build up.

- Balsamic, apple cider, rice, raspberry, and red wine Salad dressings made from them are wonderful.
- Low-sodium barbecue sauce
- Nonfat or reduced-fat mayonnaise
- Reduced-sodium ketchup
- Salt-reduced soy sauce
- Whole grain, honey, Dijon, and yellow mustard

Reduce your consumption of butter in your cooking. Use healthy oils instead, such as canola and olive.

- Alternatives to fat in baking, such as yogurt, applesauce, or fruit puree
- Cooking sprays without fat
- Margarine without trans fats
- Nonfat or reduced-fat salad dressings
- Olive and canola oils
- Shortening without hydrogen

For snacks and meals, fill your cupboard with nuts, dried fruit, and whole-wheat items.

- Baked tortilla chips without trans fats
- Brown rice cakes or popcorn cakes
- Dehydrated fruits

- Plain or light microwave popcorn
- Raw nuts and seeds, a variety (almonds, walnuts, sunflower seeds, sesame seeds)
- Trans-fat-free, whole-grain crackers
- Whole-grain pitas, tortillas, and bread
- Whole-grain pretzels

Salt versus spices: Too much salt raises blood pressure. Instead, use zingy spices and herbs to create flavor. Options consist of:

- Allspice
- Basil
- Bay leaves
- Cayenne
- Chili flakes
- Cinnamon
- Cloves
- Coriander
- Cumin
- Curry paste
- Dill
- Five-spice from China
- Flakes of red pepper
- Garlic flakes
- Ginger
- Marjoram
- Mint
- Nutmeg
- Oregano
- Paprika
- Parsley
- Powdered onion

- Rosemary
- Seasonings devoid of sodium
- Seeds from caraway
- Seasonings from Italy
- Thyme

Reduce your consumption of sugar. It is packed with calories that cause weight gain. Instead, use healthier alternatives to sate your sweet appetite; however, the less sweetness you use, the better.

- Honey (in moderation)
- Light or sugar-free maple syrups
- Using brown rice syrup in place of sugar when baking

Your Low-Sodium Diet's Game Plan for Grocery Shopping

List of Foods to buy for a low-sodium diet

Have you ever gone shopping without a list? You could even arrive at the narrative hungry. That's how you bring home meals, snacks, and desserts that aren't heart-healthy or low in salt.

Has it already been done?

Not to worry. There is never a bad moment to start eating better. Use the Grocery-Shopping Game Plan the next time you need to make a few quick shop runs. The following information can help you choose low-sodium options:

. . .

Veggies and fruits

There's a strong chance you need to eat more. According to health experts, adults should consume 1-2 cups of fruit and around 2-3 cups of veggies daily. Here are a few excellent choices:

- Fruit, fresh or frozen. Your favorite(s) (apples, oranges, bananas, pineapple, etc.)
- Fruit in cans without sugar or syrup
- Low-sodium veggies in cans.
- Veggies, either frozen or fresh. There are many options, so try broccoli, cauliflower, carrots, spinach, and peppers.

Whole grains

Avoid bread, pasta, cereals, and anything else prepared with refined grains or white flour. You're seeking products produced with whole grains, such as:

- Barley, quinoa, wild rice, or brown rice
- Oatmeal and cereal with whole grains
- Salt-free popcorn
- Whole-grain crackers, muffins, bread, and tortillas
- Whole-wheat pasta

High-protein foods

Can you still eat meat on a low-sodium diet?

Yes. However, it would help if you avoid highly processed meats and meats that are heavy in saturated fat. Instead, the following are some sensible store options:

- Fish
- Lean pork or beef
- Skinless turkey or chicken

Eggs and beans are two other alternatives for a nutritious protein.

Dairy

Do you plan to buy milk or other dairy products? Avoid dairy products that are rich in saturated fat and salt. Additionally, choose low-sodium and low-fat foods for:

- Cheese
- Cheese curds
- Milk
- Yogurt

Condiments, dressings, sauces, and oils

Many must realize how much salt is in salad dressings, sauces, oils, and condiments. Next time, look at the nutrition label. For instance, two tablespoons of soy sauce contain roughly 1,800 mg of salt.

But medical professionals advise taking no more than 2,300 mg of salt daily. Additionally, if you already have high blood pressure, consume less salt than 1,500 mg.

Use the following to season, cook, or put anything on your food:

- Ketchup with less sodium
- Margarine without salt (soft tub or liquid spread)
- Olive oil
- Salad dressings low in salt
- Sauces low in salt

Seasonings

Perhaps you used to salt your meals before each meal. But if you're attempting to safeguard your health, keep your blood sugar under control, and maintain a healthy heart, avoid the salt shaker. Instead, season your dish with these items:

- Ginger
- Limes or lemon juice
- Minced or chopped onions or garlic
- Spices and herbs

Don't worry if it seems like a lot to consider the next time you visit the grocery shop. We have your back. Choose your preferred Low-Sodium dishes from the menu, and we'll take care of the rest.

A List Of Foods To Eat With Little Or No Salt Is Available.

Shop outside the grocery store as a simple rule of thumb for selecting items with less salt. Fruits, vegetables, dairy goods, poultry, meat, and eggs may all be found there. Shopping in the inner aisles, where processed, packaged goods lure you with high salt content, fats, and sugar, should be done carefully. Whole foods and lightly processed meals all have very little or no salt.

Veggies and fruits

With very few exceptions, all fruits and vegetables are salt-free in their raw, unprocessed condition. Some food is classified as sodium free because it has so little salt. Contrarily, canned goods are often processed with salt added; even low-salt veggies and beans contain more salt than the average person would need. The following are some examples of foods that are thought to be sodium-free fruits and vegetables:

- Asparagus
- Avocados
- Bananas
- Blueberries
- Corn
- Cucumbers
- Green beans
- Eggplant
- Oranges
- Peaches
- Potatoes
- Romaine greens
- Squash in summer
- Strawberries

Chicken and meat

If you pick which goods to purchase to decrease salt, you may find plenty of nutritious protein in beef, pig, chicken, and other meats and poultry. They can also be low-sodium options. Processed foods with high salt content include deli meats, ham, and bacon. To determine if the food was processed in a saline brine, carefully read the labels on the front and back of the chicken or beef packaging. From the following goods, pick:

- fresh poultry that hasn't been brined in salt
- items made from fresh, unprocessed pork, such as pork tenderloin
- raw, fresh beef products
- recent fish

Dairy and Egg Products

There are barely 70 mg of salt in a whole giant egg. Although dairy products do not inherently have low amounts of sodium, you may reduce your salt intake if you watch your portion sizes and choose low-sodium choices. Dairy products with low salt levels have no more than 140 mg per serving.

Grains

Most grains, including brown rice, white rice, bulgur, quinoa, and oatmeal, have a little salt in their natural condition. Buy the unprocessed kinds of those items instead of processed ones like microwaveable popcorn, pretzels, quick oatmeal packaged in packets, and other processed grains that may have much more salt.

Fats

Unsaturated fats benefit a healthy diet since they are rich in important fatty acids and vitamin E. Fortunately, many foods containing these fats also have relatively low salt content. For instance, a few healthy oils that are sodium-free in terms of salt content include canola oil, olive oil, and almond oil.

Processed Foods

It's hard to avoid highly salted manufactured meals in everyday life. However, the damage might be diminished if you read labels to determine how much salt is in each meal. Pick one of the following foods:

- Froze-dried veggies without dressing
- Foodstuffs with the lowest salt content possible for that category of cuisine, such as cold cereals or spaghetti sauces
- Items that belong within the deficient sodium category and have a sodium content of 35 milligrams or less per serving on the label.
- Low-sodium versions of any product, including cereals, broths, bread, cheese, and sauces, as well as canned beans

To help you pick low-salt foods, read the labels. Use liberal amounts of fresh herbs and spices while cooking to enhance flavor without salt.

. . .

Final Thoughts

The American Heart Association recommends two meals of fish per week for those who consume meat, poultry, fish, and meat substitutes. Beans, whole grains, soups, and sauces can help decrease cholesterol by reducing salt and using healthy oils. Low-sodium options include vegetables, fruits, whole grains, high-protein foods, dairy, condiments, dressings, sauces, and oils. Shop outside the grocery store for items with less salt, such as fruits, vegetables, dairy goods, poultry, meat, and eggs. Avoid processed foods with a lot of salt in them. Low-sodium foods can help reduce salt intake, such as fresh poultry, grains, fats, and processed foods.

The key features in this chapter

- Proper heart-healthy items in your kitchen are the first step towards healthy eating.
- Reduce your consumption of butter in your cooking.
- Choose your preferred Low-Sodium dishes from the menu, and we'll take care of the rest.
- Although dairy products do not inherently have low sodium, you may reduce your salt intake by watching your portion sizes and choosing low sodium.
- To help you pick low-salt foods, read the labels.

7

EXERCISE & SALT: IS SALT IMPORTANT IN WORKOUTS?

O ver the last several years, salt has been the topic of a contentious dispute. Although the consequences of exceeding our daily recommended salt consumption are becoming more well-known, many of us are unaware that having too little salt in our bodies may also be detrimental. This is something we'll cover in much more depth shortly. We consulted our on-staff nutritionist and personal trainer for her opinion on salt and exercise and its role in your exercise routine. However, let's go right to some unflinching realities regarding salt.

Recap: what makes salt deadly?

Our blood pressure increases when we overeat salt because more water is retained within our bodies and cells. Your blood pressure rises when you consume more salt. Your heart may experience a great deal of strain from high blood pressure, which can also impact your arteries, kidneys, and brain. Long-term maintenance of high blood pressure may result in dementia, heart attacks, renal disease, strokes, and kidney failure.

BUT why is salt beneficial to you?

Salt is a good source of sodium, which is necessary for human existence. The content of our body fluids, which are continually in a delicate balance, is regulated by salt. It facilitates the absorption of all the essential nutrients by our cells and is necessary for normal muscle and nerve function. However, it would help if you watched your salt intake closely to prevent overconsumption.

Depending on your age, there are different daily salt recommendations. The NHS's suggested recommendations are shown below:

- Salt consumption of 6 grams per day is advised for those aged 11 and above and adults. This is equivalent to around one teaspoon and has 2.4g of sodium.
- It is recommended that children under 10 ingest no more than 5 grams of salt each day.
- Children age four to six should take no more than 3g of salt daily.
- Children aged one to three should take no more than 2g of salt daily.
- Babies under a year old shouldn't get more than 1g of salt daily. Breastfeeding babies will get the necessary quantities, and formula milk has comparable levels.

How are salt and exercise related to one another?

Anyone who frequently exercises at the gym is familiar with the salty taste of sweat. Although it's a brilliant technique for our bodies to cool down, we lose salt during exercise. Carly Tierney, DW's resident health and nutritional expert, discusses how low amounts of salt in your body might impair your workout:

"Salt is an essential component of our bodies, and it may aid in controlling blood volume, neuronal activity, and muscular contraction. Additionally, it maintains the fluid balance in your body. Low sodium levels may result in organ failure, muscular cramping, and dehydration. A mix of healthy meals or snacks and electrolyte-rich beverages may be better for maintaining sodium levels if an athlete is sweating a lot and losing a lot of sodium. In addition to being well-hydrated throughout your exercise and even after you leave the gym, Carly's remarks emphasize how crucial it is to maintain normal internal salt levels.

Eating salt and exercising

Although there is a suggested daily sodium intake, Carly emphasizes that it might be risky to generalize how much salt individuals should ingest. This is especially true for athletes who need to eat more to compensate for the salt they lose while exercising.

Everybody is unique; some individuals may need more salt than others based on their body size and form. It is generally advised to maintain your levels after strenuous exercise.

. . .

"The typical gym-goer may sweat off around one liter every hour of activity. Carly said that if you have been working hard, this amount might rise to two liters.

For instance, many runners experience significant salt loss during training and competition, and this causes a desire for salt after exercise. Eat a salty snack and drink a sports drink to satisfy the appetite and compensate for the loss. The recommended salt intake is 200 mg to keep the balance.

Sodium intake during exercise: is it the key? Salt and cramps?

Master trainer and nutritional specialist Eddy Diget are. He collaborates with various high-performance athletes, all of whom are required to follow a rigorous nutritional regimen that is balanced and contains the proper amounts of all nutrients. If you like your science to be supported by actual case studies, then this is the one for you:

Eddy informed us, "I have been training an 'Ultra Tri' athlete who is supposed to run for more than 100 kilometers. He had "mid-exercise cramps," so I advised him to drink 2 to 3 cc of water per pound of body weight four hours before his workout. He drank around 300–450 cc of water since he weighed 68 kg. He took a glass of water with a pinch of salt in it 15 minutes after each exercise, and he hasn't had any cramps or migraines since.

Not only that, but the NHS cautions that low levels of water in the body may cause the salt reserves to decline, which can cause, you guessed it, muscular cramps.

. . .

How to resolve a sensational low sodium diet

Although it has been shown that salt is a crucial component of our diet and is more closely related to physical activity than previously believed, we still need to restrict our consumption.

You should be aware that you're receiving your daily recommended salt intake since up to 75% is believed to come from common meals. That's even before many of us season our meals with salt at the dinner table, often out of habit. Of all, eating too much salt is simple since it lurks in areas we least expect to find.

What Sodium Does During Exercise

Sportspeople are claimed to need sodium, and several justifications are offered for why this is the case. The info-graphic below will provide a brief overview of the analysis before we go further into the facts.

Sodium serves several crucial functions during exercise. First, sodium is a key component of the balance of water. It does this because of how it affects the extracellular fluid's osmolality (fluid in the bloodstream and surrounding the outside of cells). The quantity of dissolvable particles in the liquid in it is dissolved is known as osmolality. The majority of the particles in the extracellular fluid in the body are contributed by salt. Hyponatremia, or a decrease in blood sodium levels, decreases osmolality, which may harm fluid balance. Fluids will migrate into tissues to balance the osmolality between the inside and outside of cells if the blood's sodium content falls. One of those tissues is the brain, which may experience swelling and death.

· · ·

However, this condition needs both low osmolalities to allow water to enter the cells and high overall water levels to cause the cells to swell to lethal levels. Therefore, even if this is uncommon, it is crucial to maintain a healthy salt level in the blood.

Does salt make water absorbent more quickly?

Sodium is often included in exercise beverages (carbohydrate-electrolyte or sports drinks). The addition of salt and carbohydrates to these beverages is done for a variety of reasons. A small amount of glucose will boost salt absorption, and water will follow the sodium and glucose due to osmotic drag. Although it is sometimes stated or indicated that salt aids in water absorption, this impact is little. I want to provide you with the findings from one of our studies to highlight this. This investigation added various salt concentrations to a 6% glucose solution.

Sodium enhances the flavor of beverages and encourages drinking.

Drinks often taste better when they are higher in sodium. Because increased blood osmolality causes thirst, sodium also maintains that reaction, which encourages drinking. Athletes are thus more prone to drink, which is necessary for keeping hydrated. It is crucial to remember that we only need minimal levels of electrolytes to make a drink more delicious. Drinks with 400–500 mg of salt per liter or less will be more pleasant than those with more than 1000 mg.

· · ·

Beverage osmolality is increased by sodium.

I want to draw attention to the influence of electrolytes on the osmolality of the fluids we consume. Many proponents of electrolytes also feel that osmolality plays a significant part in their understanding of electrolytes, even though the effects of osmolality on beverages and, ultimately, stomach content may be overstated in many circumstances. These people often spend a lot of money on isotonic drinks (those with an osmolality comparable to blood), which they then complement with salt pills or electrolyte tabs. These pills will drastically increase osmolality, negating any minor possible benefit from isotonic beverages.

Water retention and pre-exercise sodium levels

Last but not least, salt helps the body's water reservoirs hold onto the water that has been consumed. In essence, salt will aid the body's ability to retain water. Although there is a potential advantage, there must be more proof that it can improve performance in most circumstances.

Only research conducted in highly humid and hot settings provides data (often with minimal wind cooling). In these experiments, preloading water with sodium and other solutes, such as glycerol, improved temperature control during exercise. However, this situation is distinct from using an electrolyte solution while exercising. Preloading trials generally begin 2 hours before the workout with a significant dosage of salt or glycerol and a substantial amount of water (2-3L).

Theories as to why sodium is essential

The two basic ideas and presumptions on which the justification for supplementing with sodium is based are that you lose a lot of sodium when exercising (this is often an assumption), so:

1. Blood sodium concentrations might change or
2. The body's sodium stocks are impacted, compromising sodium's other functions

In conclusion, salt does not significantly aid in water absorption from beverages (glucose is much more important for this). However, salt will enhance the flavor of a drink and increase your thirst. Because of this, you are more likely to consume liquids, which will naturally aid in keeping you hydrated (although you generally don't need salt pills for this; just adding modest quantities of sodium to a drink may be more helpful). The function of sodium in maintaining fluid balance throughout distinct bodily compartments is its more significant impact (particularly the intra- and extracellular space).

How Much Is Sodium Lost While Working Out?

Sodium is often seen as harmful, mainly if you consume too much of it via salty meals. However, for human bodies to work effectively, salt is necessary. Here are some tips on ensuring you're getting enough salt while exercising and without getting too much.

Tip

Genetics, degree of fitness, food, the concentration of sodium in sweat, and surroundings are just a few variables that affect how much sodium you lose when exercising. For every pound of sweat lost during an exercise, you lose, on average, 500 milligrams of salt.

Effects of Sodium on Health

In particular, your body needs a set amount of salt to maintain blood pressure, blood volume, and muscle usage. But while you sweat during strenuous exercise, you also lose significant salt.

Although sodium is sometimes referred to be a bad component of certain meals, human bodies need a specific level of salt to thrive. The American Heart Association states that you need at least 500 milligrams of salt daily to sustain key biological processes, such as muscular contraction, nerve impulse transmission, and fluid balance.

It's uncommon for someone to take just 500 mg of salt daily, and one bagel has about 500 mg of salt, so you can see how that fits into the typical American diet. Although Americans generally consume more than 3,400 mg of salt daily, the American Heart Association advises against exceeding 2,300 milligrams. It is not unexpected that the American diet is rich in salt, given that it is full of processed meats, bread, and cheeses.

The health risks of consuming such high salt levels are real. Your kidneys strive to keep your body's sodium level balanced, but if it increases excessively, it ends up in your blood and causes high blood pressure. The American Heart Association also points out that consuming too much salt has been connected to weight gain, migraines, renal illness, heart issues, and stroke.

Additionally, it is widely accepted that too much salt is bad for every organ in the body. Too much salt is bad for blood vessels, the heart, the kidneys, and the brain, according to a November 2016 research published in the Journal of the American College of Cardiology.

Loss of Sodium During Exercise

You must thus sweat once daily to exercise and keep your salt levels in check. It takes a lot of work, physical activity, and sweat to shed a significant. Sweating causes you to lose electrolytes and water while you work out, and sweating is the primary route for salt loss during exercise. According to MedlinePlus, electrolytes are minerals with an electric charge in your blood, tissues, and bodily fluids, and they regulate your body's water levels, pH levels, nutrients, and cell waste.

In addition to sodium, electrolytes you get through food and beverages include calcium, potassium, phosphate, magnesium, and sodium. Dehydration, or the loss of bodily fluids, may occur if you sweat too quickly and don't consume enough water.

Researchers have been investigating salt loss during exercise for a long time, but it may be challenging to detect. According to a March 2017 research published in Sports Medicine, it's critical to determine how much an athlete sweats and loses sodium over training time. This may help them determine how much they need to replace fluids, electrolytes, and salt.

· · ·

Factors for Salt Loss

For every pound of sweat, you produce, you'll lose, on average, 500 milligrams of salt. However, this will vary from person to person since various variables, including genetics, body weight, food, and heat acclimation, influence sweating.

The surroundings and heat also play a significant part. Running a long distance in the summer heat can cause you to sweat more and lose more sodium than a brisk stroll in the winter, so you'll need to rehydrate by eating and drinking enough sodium and electrolytes.

However, suppose you're exercising 30 minutes a day at the gym, working a desk job, and generally leading a sedentary lifestyle. In that case, your sodium loss during exercise may not justify a low-sodium diet, and exercise and sweating to purge your body of extra salt may thus not always be practical. A significant element is also a balanced diet.

Low-Sodium Meals

It would help if you modified your diet to balance your salt levels and maintain them healthy in addition to your regular exercises or outdoor physical activity in the heat. Even if you avoid all salty fast food and processed foods and stick to a balanced diet of fresh meats, fruits, and vegetables, you'll still be taking in more sodium than you need.

The majority of foods, including milk, celery, and even certain forms of drinking water, naturally contain sodium, and it may also be found in table salt or Himalayan salt. Many items, like soy sauce, bacon, and canned soups, not only naturally contain sodium but also have salt added to them.

· · ·

Most packaged and processed items, such as cookies, baked goods, deli meats, chips, and frozen dinners, must be avoided if you want a low-sodium diet. Your body only needs around one-fourth teaspoon of table salt per day, which may be readily obtained naturally in meats, vegetables, and dairy products, and some salt for flavoring meals, if that clarifies things.

Pick foods low in salt, such as fish, meats, fresh fruit and vegetables, nuts, and legumes. Remove the salt shaker from your table and season your meal imaginatively instead of using olive oil, crushed red pepper, vinegar, garlic, lemon, ginger, or spices if you're still concerned about your salt consumption.

Final Thoughts

Although salt is a good source of sodium, consuming too much of it can increase blood pressure and cause dementia, heart attacks, strokes, renal disease, and kidney failure. Salt is an essential component of our bodies, and low levels can lead to organ failure, muscular cramping, and dehydration. It is necessary to maintain normal internal salt levels. Eddy Diget advises athletes to drink 2-3 cc of water per pound of body weight four hours before exercise to prevent muscle cramps. Sodium is a critical component of water balance and can affect fluid balance.

Maintaining a healthy salt level in the blood during exercise is essential. Sodium enhances the flavor of beverages and encourages drinking, but it only needs minimal levels of electrolytes to make them more delicious. Sodium is necessary for water retention and pre-exercise sodium levels, but there is little proof that it can improve performance. It does not significantly aid in water absorption from beverages, but it enhances flavor and increases thirst. Gaining excess weight and experiencing headaches, kidney disease, heart problems, and stroke are all adverse effects of consuming too much salt.

Sweating is the primary route for salt loss during exercise, but it can vary from person to person due to genetics, body weight, food, and heat acclimation. Low-sodium diets require a modified diet to balance salt and maintain healthy levels, avoiding fast food and processed foods.

The key features in this chapter

- Salt is an essential component of our bodies.
- It is generally advised to maintain your levels after strenuous exercise.
- The recommended salt intake is 200 mg.
- Sodium is a key component of the balance of water.
- The health risks of consuming such high salt levels are accurate.
- The American Heart Association also points out that consuming too much salt has been connected to weight gain, migraines, renal illness, heart issues, and stroke.
- It is widely accepted that too much salt is bad for every organ in the body.
- The primary route for salt loss during exercise is sweating.
- You need to modify your diet to balance out your salt levels and maintain them healthy in addition to your regular exercises or outdoor physical activity in the heat.
- Most packaged and processed items, such as cookies, baked goods, deli meats, chips, and frozen dinners, must be avoided if you want a low-sodium diet.

FOOD ANALYSIS

The following foods **are likely to be high in salt**, along with alternative suggestions.

Baked Food

Baked beans

In contrast to other canned beans, baked beans cannot be rinsed with water to remove part of the salt since doing so would also remove the tasty sauce. Baked beans with sauce contain 524 mg of sodium, or 23% of the RDI, in a 1/2 cup (127-gram) portion. Even though homemade baked bean recipes may not have less sodium, you may adjust them to add less salt.

Macaroni and cheese

This popular comfort dish has a lot of sodium, mainly from the salty cheese sauce. A recent investigation, however, indicates that manufacturers may have reduced the salt content of macaroni and cheese by 10% on average.

According to recent research, the dry mix needed to produce a 1-cup (189-gram) portion of macaroni and cheese typically contains 475 mg of salt or 20% of the RDI.Consider choosing a whole-grain macaroni and cheese and thinning the dish by adding veggies, such as broccoli or spinach, if you only want to consume this food.

Pizza

Nearly half of the salt consumed by Americans comes from pizza and other multi-ingredient foods. The salt content of several components, including cheese, sauce, dough, and processed meat, rapidly increases when mixed.

The average amount of salt in a big, 140-gram piece of frozen pizza is 765 mg or 33% of the RDI. The salt content of a similar-sized slice from a restaurant is much higher, averaging 957 mg, or 41% of the RDI. If you consume more slices, the salt soon accumulates. Limit your intake to one slice and finish your meal with low-sodium items, such as a leafy green salad with a low-sodium dressing.

Boxed Meals

Boxed meal assistance

Meal aids in boxes often include spaghetti or similar carbohydrate, spices, and sauce in powder form. You usually add water and browned ground beef on the stovetop, or sometimes chicken or fish. The downside is that the salt content of a regular 1/4 to 1/2 cup (30 to 40 grams) of dry mix is 575 mg or 25% of the RDI. Making your stir-fry recipe using lean meat, chicken, and frozen veggies is considerably healthier and still speedy.

· · ·

Boxed potato casseroles

Scalloped potatoes and other cheesy potato recipes from boxes include a lot of salt. Some also contain preservatives and salt from MSG. 450 mg of sodium, or 19% of the RDI, is included in a 1/2-cup (27-gram) serving of dry scalloped potato mix, which yields a 2/3-cup cooked meal. Everyone would benefit more if they switched from packaged potatoes to other nutrient-dense carbohydrates like roasted sweet potatoes or winter squash.

Kinds of Bread

Bagels and other bread

Although the salt content of bread, buns, and dinner rolls is usually relatively high, it may build up if a person consumes multiple servings daily. Due to their propensity for being enormous, bagels provide much more salt than other foods. One bagel from the grocery store has 400 mg of salt, 17% of the RDI. You may reduce your salt intake by eating less bread; whole-grain varieties are better.

Biscuits

Even without gravy, this popular breakfast item has a fair amount of salt. Biscuits should only be consumed seldom since they may contain particularly high levels of salt if made from frozen or chilled dough.

One biscuit produced from packaged dough had an average salt content in the US of 528 mg or 23% of the RDI. Nevertheless, some included up to 840 mg of salt, or 36% of the RDI, in each meal.

.   .   .

Bread

A 2011 research claimed that certain loaves of bread might have the same amount of salt in each slice as a bag of crisps.

Pretzels

Your first indication of the sodium level in pretzels comes from the huge salt crystals on top of them.Pretzels typically contain 322 mg of sodium per 1-ounce (28-gram) serving or 14% of the RDI.

Although unsalted pretzels are available, they shouldn't be your go-to snack since they are often prepared with white flour and provide no nutrients.

Sandwiches

Another multi-ingredient food that accounts for over half of the salt Americans eat is the sandwich.The often-used bread, processed meat, cheese, and condiments significantly increase the salt content of sandwiches. For instance, a 6-inch cold-cut submarine sandwich typically contains 1,127 mg sodium, or 49% of the RDI. You may drastically reduce your salt intake by selecting unprocessed sandwich toppings, such as grilled chicken breast with sliced avocado and tomato.

Tortillas

The majority of the sodium in tortillas comes from salt and leaveners like baking soda or baking powder. The average amount of salt in an 8-inch (55-gram) flour tortilla is 391 mg or 17% of the RDI. So, if you eat two soft-shell tacos, the tortillas will provide one-third of your daily recommended salt intake. If you like tortillas, choose whole grain varieties and consider how the salt content compares to your recommended daily intake.

Canned and Instant Foods

Canned vegetables

Although handy, canned veggies include a fair amount of salt. For instance, 310 mg of sodium, or 13% of the RDI, is included in a 1/2 cup (124 grams) meal of canned peas. Asparagus in cans has a salt content of 346 mg per 1/2 cup (122-gram serving), or 15% of the RDI. Depending on the produce, draining and washing canned vegetables for a few minutes may lower the salt level by 9–23%. Alternately, use simple, frozen veggies, which are handy and low in salt.

Cereal

You may anticipate that certain cereal brands would have a lot of sugar, but it has been discovered that many of the most common versions also include a staggering amount of salt.

Instant pudding

Even though pudding doesn't taste salty, the quick pudding mix contains a lot of sodium.

The source of this sodium is salt, with the sodium-containing thickening agents' disodium phosphate and tetrasodium pyrophosphate that thicken the instant pudding. 350 mg of sodium, or 15% of the RDI, may be found in a 25-gram serving of instant vanilla pudding mix, which produces a 1/2 cup. In comparison, 135 mg, or 6% of the RDI, of salt is included in the same quantity of ordinary vanilla pudding mix.

Dairy

Cheddar Cheese

Already heavy in saturated fats, it was discovered that 95% of cheese products included more salt per serving than a package of pre-salted crisps.

Cottage cheese

The amount of salt in cottage cheese is relatively high, even though it is an excellent source of protein and calcium. Cottage cheese typically contains 350 mg of salt per 1/2 cup (113 grams) or 15% of the RDI (13). In addition to enhancing taste and contributing to texture, salt is a preservative in cottage cheese. Therefore, low-sodium versions are often not available. But according to one research, draining cottage cheese after 3 minutes of washing under running water reduces the salt level by 63%.

Processed cheese

Processed cheeses, such as pre-sliced American cheese and processed cheese that resembles a loaf, like Velveeta, often contain more salt than natural cheese. This is partially due to emulsifying salts, including sodium phosphate, which provides a consistent, smooth result when processed cheese is produced at high temperatures.

Compared to loaf cheese, which contains 444 mg of

sodium per 1-ounce (28-gram) portion, 16% more than the RDI for sodium, American cheese has 377 mg, or 16% less.

Instead, use natural cheeses with less salt, such as mozzarella or Swiss.

Dried and Frozen Foods

Bratwurst and hot dogs

A hot dog or bratwurst link had an average salt content of 578 mg, or 25% of the RDI, in a recent survey of packaged goods from the US. However, the salt content of the sample of these processed meats varied from 230 to 1,330 mg, which implies that if you carefully read labels, you could discover lower-sodium choices. However, saving processed meats for special occasions is advisable rather than eating them often. The World Health Organization (WHO) warned that consuming processed meats puts you at risk for developing certain malignancies.

Frozen meals

The salt content of many frozen meals is considerable; some have at least half of your daily sodium allowance in each serving. Since salt levels within a single product line may vary considerably, read the labels of each variation carefully. According to the FDA, a frozen meal must contain no more than 600 mg of salt to be considered healthy. You may use this figure as a realistic salt limit when buying frozen meals. Still, cooking your food is healthier.

Jerky and other dried meats

Jerky and other dried meats are portable and a good source of protein, but salt is used frequently to preserve them and give them a taste.

For instance, one ounce (28 grams) of beef jerky contains 620 mg sodium, or 27% of the RDI.

If you like jerky, try to choose meat from animals that were reared organically or on grass-fed diets since they tend to have shorter ingredient lists and lower salt content. However, be careful to read the label.

Salami and cold cuts

Cold cuts, often known as luncheon meats and salami, not only have a high salt content, but many are also produced with sodium-rich preservatives and other chemicals. Cold cuts typically contain 497 mg of sodium per 55-gram (2-ounce) portion or 21% of the RDI. The exact quantity of salami has 1,016 mg, or 44% of the RDI, which is significantly greater.

Fresh, sliced meats like roast beef or turkey are better alternatives.

Meat, Poultry, Seafood

Ham

Ham contains a lot of sodium because salt is required to season and cure the meat. Roasted ham typically includes 1,117 mg of sodium per 3-ounce (85-gram) meal or 48% of the RDI. Food manufacturers need to reduce how salty they salt this popular meat. Researchers recently discovered that ham had a 14% greater salt content than in the prior investigation after sampling items throughout the country. Instead of

consuming a whole ham dish, think about using it sometimes as a little condiment.

Meat, poultry, and seafood in cans

Canned meats have a greater salt content than fresh
equivalents, like other canned foods. However, some
producers may be progressively lowering sodium. In a
recent study, canned tuna has 10% of the recommended
daily intake (RDI) or 247 mg of salt per 3-ounce (85-gram)
portion. The salt concentration decreased by 27% compared
to a few decades ago. Per a recent study, a 3-ounce (85-gram)
meal, or 9–18% of the RDI, canned chicken or turkey had
212-425 mg of salt. The salt content of cured, canned meats,
such as corned beef and pig, was much higher (794–1,393 mg
of sodium, or 29–51% of the RDI) per 3-ounce (85-gram)
portion.

Instead, choose fresh foods or canned goods with less
salt.

Pork rinds

The popularity of crispy pig rinds (skins) has soared as
interest in the low-carb ketogenic diet has expanded. Pork
rinds are a keto-friendly snack but include a lot of salt. Pork
rinds include 515 mg of sodium in a 1-ounce (28-gram)
portion or 22% of the RDI. Choosing the barbecue flavor
will result in a serving containing 747 mg of salt, or 32% of
the RDI. Consider unsalted nuts if you're yearning for something crispy instead.

Salt pork, bacon, and sausage

Sausage typically contains 415 mg of salt per 2-ounce (55-gram) portion, or 18% of the RDI, whether in links or patties. Bacon contains 233 mg of sodium per 1-ounce (28-gram) serving or 10% of the RDI. Check the nutrition label since turkey bacon might have just as much salt. A 1-ounce (28-gram) portion of salt pork, used to flavor foods like baked beans and clam chowder, contains almost twice the fat of bacon and 399 mg of sodium, or 17% of the RDI. Regardless of the salt content, it would help if you consume these processed meats in moderation for your health.

Shrimp

Preservatives high in sodium are often added to packaged, plain, frozen shrimp for taste. Sodium tripolyphosphate, for instance, is often added to reduce moisture loss during thawing. As much as 800 mg of sodium, or 35% of the RDI, may be found in a 3-ounce (85-gram) frozen, unbreaded shrimp meal. Similarly, salty shrimp is breaded and fried. In comparison, a serving of fresh, caught shrimp that is 3 ounces (85 grams) in size and devoid of salt and other seasonings contains only 101 mg of sodium or 4% of the RDI. If possible, choose freshly caught shrimp. You may also look for additive-free frozen shrimp at a health food shop.

Salad, Sauces & Soups

Salad dressing

Salt is a source of some of the sodium in salad dressing. In addition, some products use sodium-rich flavorings, such as MSG and its relatives, disodium inosinate and disodium guanylate. Salad dressing averaged 304 mg of salt per 2-tablespoon (28-gram) portion in an assessment of popular brand-name goods available in US shops, which is 13% of the RDI. However, the salad dressing samples varied in salt content from 10-620 mg per serving, so you can locate a low-sodium option if you shop carefully.

Making your own is an even better choice. Utilize vinegar and extra virgin olive oil.

Sauces

When preparing or serving food, sauces may add taste, but part of that flavor comes from salt.

A 1-tablespoon (15-ml) portion of soy sauce has 1,024 mg of sodium, or 44% of the RDI, making it one of the saltiest condiments. The salt in barbecue sauce is also reasonably high; 2 teaspoons (30 ml) contain 395 mg of sodium or 17% of the RDI. To keep levels low, you can either manufacture your sauces, such as soy sauce, or purchase reduced-sodium versions of certain sauces.

Soup

Although there are reduced-sodium alternatives for certain canned kinds, canned, packaged, and restaurant-prepared soups often include a lot of salt. Although some soups also include sodium-rich flavorings such as monosodium glutamate, salt is the primary source of sodium in these dishes (MSG). Per 1-cup (245-gram) serving, canned soup typically contains 700 mg sodium or 30% of the RDI.

. . .

Stocks and broths

Known for having a high salt content, packaged broths, and stocks are often used as the foundation for soups and stews or to flavor meat and vegetable dishes. For instance, a serving of 8 ounces (240 mL) of beef broth typically contains 782 mg of sodium or 34% of the RDI. Both chicken and vegetable broths contain a lot of salt. Fortunately, obtaining broths and stocks with less sodium than standard versions is simple—at least 25% less sodium per serving.

Stock Cubes

Who would have thought this little flavor-enhancing cube would be on our list? However, some of them contain as much as 50% salt.

Tinned Soup

Thought to be a healthy lunch choice by many, it may not be. Studies have revealed that certain canned soups may contain as much salt as two pieces of takeout pizza.

Tomato sauce

Checking the salt content of a can of simple tomato sauce or other canned tomato products may not occur to you, but you should. Tomato sauce contains 321 mg of salt, or 14% of the RDI, in only 1/4 cup (62 grams). Fortunately, it's easy to get canned tomato products without salt.

Vegetables

Pickles

One 1-ounce (28-gram) spear of dill pickle, which may be served with a deli sandwich, has around 241 mg of sodium, or 10% of the RDI. Whole pickles have a quicker salt buildup. 561 mg of sodium, or 24% of the RDI, may be found in one medium-sized dill pickle. If you're on a regimen that limits your salt intake, limit your intake of pickles.

Vegetable juice

Vegetable juice is a convenient way to consume vegetables, but if you don't check nutrition labels, you can also consume a lot of salt. Vegetable juice may contain 405 mg of sodium, or 17% of the RDI, in an 8-ounce (240 mL) serving. Thankfully, several manufacturers offer low-sodium alternatives, limited to 140 mg of salt per serving by FDA regulations.

Worst Fast-Food Meals

While enjoying fast food, are you conscious of your salt intake? Here are some nutritious alternatives for those foods rich in salt. Although fast food is quick, it may be salty and is saltier in the United States than in other nations. More than double the daily limit of 1,500 mg for those over 50, African Americans, and those with hypertension, diabetes, or renal illness, the typical American takes 3,400 mg of salt daily.

Although eating fast food sometimes won't ruin anyone's diet, you should restrict salt, advises Rima Kleiner, RD, a nutritionist based in Greensboro, North Carolina.

Here are some of the worst fast-food dishes that made our list of salty foods and their more nutritious substitutes.

2/3-lb Monster Thickburger from Hardee's

This 2-patty monster is a meat lover's worst food nightmare. It includes 1,300 calories, 93 grams of fat, and 2,860 mg of sodium, with three slices of American cheese and four pieces of bacon, and that doesn't include fries or a Coke. A double cheeseburger is a better alternative, and it's meaty and cheesy and has fewer calories (410), fat (21 grams), and salt than other similar dishes (900 mg).

Arby's Mozzarella Sticks

Six battered and fried sticks include more than a day's worth of salt, 2,530 mg, and 620 calories. The saltiest cheese is sometimes whole-milk mozzarella, and according to CalorieLab.com, it has 178 mg of salt per ounce, compared to over 272 mg for a Kraft nonfat American single. According to Kleiner, the breading mixture often contains a lot of salt, which raises the sodium level of the fried mozzarella sticks. Instead, choose this: Three Potato Cakes have 340 calories and 700 mg of salt per serving.

Big Breakfast with Hotcakes at McDonald's

Big is accurate. You get a tiny stack of pancakes, hash browns, sausage, scrambled eggs, and hash browns. You'll start the day with 1,150 calories and 2,260 mg of salt when you order it with a big biscuit. Instead, choose this: Get the Big Breakfast without the hotcakes to save 350 calories and 580 mg of salt.

. . .

Carl's Jr -½ Pound Mile High Bacon Thickburger

The thickest burger is Carl's Jr.'s 1/2 pound Mile High Bacon Thickburger. The Applewood-smoked bacon may seduce you if the 1/2-pound patty fails to do so. Although I like this burger's concept, appearance, and flavor, more than 1,230 calories for just one serving may not be worth it for someone trying to reduce their calorie consumption.

The huge beef patties and the bacon, mayonnaise, and cheese contribute to the dish's high-calorie content. Thanks to these toppings, the burger is a taste explosion but exceedingly harmful.

Chipotle's Burrito

When making a tortilla from scratch, the salt accumulates very rapidly. There are 1,185 calories and 2,650 mg of sodium in a Carnitas, or pork, burrito with white rice, pinto beans, tomatillo-red chile sauce, Romaine lettuce, sour cream, cheese, and guacamole. Unexpectedly, the soft wheat tortilla holding it all together is the saltiest component (at 670 mg of sodium).

Instead, choose this: A bowl of burritos. Instead of tortillas, dish out lower-salt ingredients such as chicken, brown rice, fajita vegetables, and green tomatillo salsa. Three hundred eighty-five calories and 920 mg of salt are the totals.

Chipotle Salad

(with sofritas, cilantro-flavored brown rice, black beans, fajita vegetables, fresh tomato salsa, guacamole, queso, roast chili corn salsa, sour cream, and ChipotleChipotle honey vinaigrette) One thousand three hundred ten calories, 75 g fat (0 g trans fat, 21.5 g saturated fat), 3,505 mg sodium, 127 g carbohydrates (26 g fiber, 31 g sugar), and 35 g protein make up the diet.

"Your order may be processed swiftly given the popularity of ChipotleChipotle and the recent trend toward plant-based diets. The above order has 1300 calories or around 3/4 of a day's worth. Despite being vegan, this dish has several high-calorie, high-fat toppings, including cheese, sour cream, and dressing. Selecting one of the three possibilities instead of all three is an immediate improvement method." — Tony Castillo, a performance dietitian with Nutrition For Performance and an MS, RD, LDN.

Cinnabon's Caramel Pecanbon

Since gooey cinnamon buns are their specialty, nothing at Cinnabon is very nutritious. But regarding harmful menu items, the Caramel Pecanbon is one of the biggest offenders. This cinnamon roll is made even more delicious and sinful by being covered with icing, caramel, and nuts.There are already a lot of 880 calories and 37 grams of fat in a single traditional Cinnabon roll. The Caramel Pecanbon, however, kicks things up with a staggering 1,090 calories and 51 grams of fat. This indicates that one cinnamon roll has over half the daily calorie allowance. In addition, you need to receive more nutrients.

. . .

Culver's Triple Bacon Deluxe Burger

One thousand ninety calories, 76 g of fat (30.5 g saturated, 2.1 g trans), 1,430 mg of sodium, 42 g of carbohydrates (1 g fiber, 9 g sugar), and 60 g of protein make up the diet. "Culver's, which hails from Wisconsin, is a mainstay of our fast food business. They provide some of the best burgers in the fast food industry. The Culver's Triple Bacon Deluxe Burger has an absurdly high-calorie count, so there is no way someone could feel good after eating it. The average American would consume more than half of their daily requirements for calories and fat from this one burger, which has 1,090 calories and 76 grams of fat." The Gorski

Dairy Queen chili cheese fries

This diet contains 990 calories, broken down into 107 g of fat, carbohydrates (9 of fiber and 4 of sugar), 25 of protein, 2,280 milligrams of sodium, and 14 of and 1 gram of trans fat. "The majority of people, in my opinion, consider "cheese fries" to be a side dish, but this is not your average serving of fries, and that's where problems might arise. This meets your daily salt limit since it has about 1,000 calories, 52 grams of fat, and 2,280 milligrams of sodium.

Domino's Mac-N-Cheese

While a gooey bowl of melted cheese and penne pasta is a welcome break from pizza, it comes with 1,760 mg of salt and 670 calories per serving. This traditional American dish in a bread bowl has 730 calories and 1,390 mg of salt per half-serving. Are you stopping after half a bowl? Try increasing the figures by two. Instead, choose this: a serving of primavera pasta. It has 540 calories and 770 mg of sodium.

. . .

Double Decker Taco Supreme from Taco Bell

The nutritional breakdown of this meal includes:

- 310 calories.
- 15 grams of fat (4.5 grams of saturated fat, 0 grams of trans fat).
- 610 milligrams of sodium.
- 34 grams of carbs (Contains 4 g of dietary fiber and 2 g of sugar).
- 11 grams of protein.

"Why do a white flour taco and a fried taco enter a bar? Why may you need both? And then fill it with ground meat, an oil-heavy sauce we don't advocate, a sprinkling of veggies, and less beef (in an era when cutting down on daily beef intake is advised)? Additionally, this food has about a third of your daily salt allowance.

Double Quarter Pounder with Cheese from McDonald's

The diet has 740 calories, 42 grams of fat (20 grams of saturated and 2.5 grams of trans fat), 1,360 milligrams of sodium, 43 grams of carbs (2 grams of fiber, 10 grams of sugar), and 48 grams of protein. The Double Quarter Pounder with Cheese from McDonald's has more calories than the Big Mac. It includes 720 calories, around 200 more than the Big Mac, and a shocking 42 grams of fat (2.5 grams of trans fat). Combined with a big fry and a large beverage, this meal may easily include more calories than most individuals need daily." The Gorski Alternatively, why choose one of The 5 Healthiest McDonald's Burgers, per a dietitian?

. . .

Double SmokeShack

This meal has 870 calories, 57 grams of fat (24 grams of saturated fat, 2 grams of trans fat), 3,030 milligrams of sodium, 28 grams of carbs (zero grams of fiber, seven grams of sugar), and 58 grams of protein. "I feel like this is a heart attack waiting to happen, with 24 grams of saturated fat and 3,030 grams of salt.

Dunkin' Donuts' Salt Bagel

Are bagels healthier than donuts? Not when "salt" is involved. The Dunkin' version has 310 calories and 3,350 mg of salt. Instead, choose this: A cinnamon-raisin bagel with 320 calories. 500 mg of sodium is present.

Five Guys – Large French Fries

Many believe that fast-food burgers are the unhealthiest options and see french fries as a harmless side dish. However, fried potatoes may be harmful, particularly if you order huge servings. With over 1,400 calories, Five Guy's big french fries are a heavyweight competitor and maybe the unhealthiest fast food item on the market! Fresh, hand-cut, and best-tasting fast food fries can are Five Guys. But unless you want to share with a large party, stick with the small size to indulge yourself.

Full Turkey Bacon Bravo from Panera Bread

The 2,800 mg of salt in this 800-calorie sandwich of smoked turkey, Applewood smoked bacon, and Gouda with lettuce and tomato on tomato basil bread. Kleiner claims processed meats and cured bacon often have significant salt content, and the salt content of the bread alone is 320 mg. Instead, choose this: a complete Panini with Roasted Turkey and Artichokes on Focaccia with Asiago Cheese. You may reduce salt consumption by over half for nearly the same amount of calories (780). (1,190 mg of sodium).

Hardee's Monster Thickburger

1/3 pound of Angus beef with fatty toppings like bacon, mayo, and cheese make up the Hardee's Monster Thickburger. This burger is as delicious as it sounds because fat is taste. However, this burger is undoubtedly on the high-calorie side at 1420 calories. This compares to around 3/4 of the daily calorie intake recommended for an average adult. Avoid ordering this burger unless you're eating a salad or other lighter, healthier meals for the remainder of the day. To enjoy this burger without going overboard, I prefer to share it with a buddy.

Jack in the Box's Deli Trio

On artisan bread, roasted turkey is stacked with ham, pickles, Provolone cheese, and salty Genoa salami. A rich Italian dressing is also spread on top. Surprise! The bread and the turkey (455 mg of sodium each) are the saltiest components (596 mg). The Deli Trio has 624 calories and 2,442 mg of salt. Instead, choose this: a Pita with Chicken Fajita. Over two-thirds will reduce your daily salt consumption to 870 mg. 320 calories.

. . .

KFC's Big Box Meal

For each item, KFC gives nutritional details. With a drumstick, a Crispy Strip, a Popcorn **Chicken** individual box, two Homestyle sides (we went with mashed potatoes with gravy and cole slaw), a biscuit, and a 32-oz, assuming you drink a can of Pepsi with your dinner, you'll get more than 1,400 calories and more than 3,000 milligrams of salt, far beyond the recommended daily. Instead, choose this: The Honey BBQ Snacker has a big ear of corn on the cob, a 16-ounce Lipton Brisk Lemon Tea, and a house side salad with buttermilk dressing. This meal contains 505 calories and 725 mg less salt than the previous one—Kleiner's advice: Dress separately. To obtain the flavor of it without all the salt, dip your fork in it.

KFC Chicken Pot Pie

Known for its delicate fried chicken, KFC is a well-known business. While no deep-fried food will benefit your health, KFC's **Chicken** Pot Pie could be better. One of the worst fast food options is this meal. Pot pies include a staggering 790 calories and 41 grams of fat per serving. Chicken pieces, veggies, and a gravy-like sauce make up the filling. Most of these calories are found in the doughy crust that covers the creamy interior. Even though it sounds mouthwatering, eating this often won't benefit you in any way.While having one or two slices of pizza may be OK, remember that most people eat more than one slice when they sit down to eat a pie, so the calories will undoubtedly pile up. I advise ordering a pizza with more vegetables and fewer types of meat. You may restrict yourself to one slice and add a delicious, full salad to your dinner.

. . .

Large Caramel Apple Pie Blizzard from Dairy Queen

One thousand two hundred calories, 48 g of fat (33 g saturated, 1.5 g trans), 550 mg of sodium, 173 g of carbohydrates (1 g fiber, 134 g sugar), and 20 g of protein make up the diet. "A total of 48 grams of fat (including 33 grams of saturated fat and 1.5 grams of trans fat) provide 1200 calories. This food item only has 20 grams of protein and 134 grams of sugar. This is perhaps the least nutritious fast food item you can buy (if I had my way, the huge size shouldn't even be offered for sale)." — Carli.

Large Sonic Sauced Popcorn Chicken with Buffalo.

Nine hundred twenty calories, 60g of fat, 11g of saturated fat, 1g of trans fat, 105mg of cholesterol, 4,670mg of sodium, 58g of carbohydrates, 8g of dietary fiber, 3g of sugar, and 37g of protein. "The amount of salt in these wings is 4,670 milligrams, or 203% of the daily limit advised by the Dietary Guidelines for Americans, which is 2,300 milligrams. This food has 540 calories, or 540 calories from fat, which is more than half of the total calories in the item. An individual's chance of having heart failure, stroke, high blood pressure, high cholesterol, etc., might rise when they consume too much salt and saturated fat. These statistics may be frightening when you imagine consuming three of them every week. Avoid this dish to maintain a healthy, powerful heart." The Valdez

Mac & cheese from Panera Bread

One thousand ten calories, 67 grams of fat (37 grams of saturated fat, 2.5 grams of trans fat), 2,220 milligrams of sodium, 67 grams of carbohydrates (2 grams of fiber, 16 grams of sugar), and 33 grams of protein. "There are more than 1000 calories, 67 grams of fat, 2220 mg of sodium, and just 2 grams of fiber in this Mac & Cheese. If you are dining out, try to order something with fiber to aid satiety since fiber may help us feel filled for longer. Consider the broccoli cheese soup instead, which has fewer calories (360), less salt (1,330 mg), and more fiber (6 grams)." It's Pankonin. 98% of Americans don't consume enough fiber, speaking of which. Thankfully, Panera offers a variety of healthy menu options, like steel-cut oats, a Caesar salad with grilled chicken, and a BLT with roasted turkey and avocado.

McDonald's Large Caramel Frappe

Six hundred eighty calories, 29g fat, 18g saturated fat, 1.5 trans fats, 85mg cholesterol, 200mg sodium, 94g carbohydrates, 0g dietary fiber, 88g sugar, and 10g protein comprise the following nutrient breakdown. Do you know how much sugar 88 grams in one drink would be? Well, accept it because it is accurate. Men should limit their daily sugar intake to 36 grams, while women should limit their intake to 25 grams, according to the American Heart Association. This McDonald's "coffee" should be avoided at all costs or used sparingly, and it tastes more like dessert.

Papa John's Pizza with Buffalo Chicken

The cheese, bacon, pizza dough, creamy ranch, and buffalo sauce are the main sources of salt in this chicken-crusted pie. One large original crust slice, or one-eighth of an order, provides 370 calories and 1,050 mg of salt. But you already know you'll eat at least two pieces. Instead, choose this: There are a ton of fresh vegetables in Papa John's

Garden Fresh. A big pie with a thin crust only has 220 calories and 360 mg of salt per piece.

Pizza Hut -Personal Meat Lover's Pizza

The Personal Meat Lover's Pizza from Pizza Hut is, as the name implies, a meat-heavy pizza.

Ingredients for the pizza include:

- pepperoni
- sausage
- ham
- beef
- bacon

There is also a double layer of cheese on the thin crust. Therefore, this pizza is calorie and fat-dense.

Popeye's Chicken Po' Boy

This classic Southern dish includes two fried chicken tenders battered and dipped in mayonnaise and pickles. This greasy, salty combination has 635 calories and 2,120 mg of sodium. You are capable of more. Instead, choose this: Unclothed Chicken Wrap. "Naked" because no breading is used in the chicken preparation, lowering the salt content to 580 mg and boosting the calorie content to 200.

Quiznos' Large French Dip

This sandwich is a salt bomb even though it looks delicious: It consists of thinly sliced prime rib, mozzarella, roasted peppers, onions, and a light peppercorn sauce on artisan bread, served with a side of au jus. If you skip the cheese, sauce, and juice, you'll still consume 2,240 milligrams. It has a staggering 3,610 mg of salt and 1,200 calories when served with the works. (850mg of sodium are added from the au jus.). Instead, choose this: Customize a flatbread. Consider pairing Swiss cheese and roast beef with lettuce, tomato, onion, and honey-dijon dressing. 995 milligrams of sodium. 410 calories.

Shake Shack's Double SmokeShack Burger

The Double SmokeShack Burger from Shake Shack is a double beef patty burger with American cheese, bacon, and delectable ShackSauce on top. Fifty-three grams of fat and 830 calories are in this burger. Even though it's wonderful, it would take roughly 240 minutes of walking to burn off that many calories. This comparison will help determine if it is delicious enough to warrant ordering. Although Shake Shack's Double SmokeShack Burger is one of their unhealthiest fast food alternatives, other delicious, healthier options are available.

For instance, if you're a vegan who enjoys fast food, try their plant-based vegetarian burger.

Sonic -SuperSonic Bacon Double Cheeseburger

As the name indicates, Sonic's SuperSonic Bacon Double Cheeseburger features two beef patties, cheese, and bacon.But there's more! It also has mayo, ketchup, mustard, lettuce, and pickles. This burger has a staggering 1,190 calories and 83 grams of fat on toasted bread. That applies to the sandwich itself! A dinner with fries and a drink will likely have over 2,000 calories.

I adore this burger. However, I usually get it without the fries and a sweet beverage on the side.

Starbucks Pumpkin Scone

Five hundred calories, 23 g of fat (14 g saturated,.5 g trans), 450 mg of salt, 70 g of carbohydrates (1 g fiber, 46 g sugar), and 4 g protein make up the diet. "46 grams of sugar aren't a party, no matter how exuberant they may seem. One croissant has 11.5 packets of sugar, and there is hardly any protein or fiber to keep you full. This is a terrible Starbucks scenario because of the white flour, sugar, butter, lack of fiber, and absence of fruit or vegetable. And that's before a drink. Although we have nothing against scones, making your own would be considerably more beneficial if you wanted to include fiber and plant-based protein." Foreigner Moreno Make sure you are aware of The 8 Healthiest Starbucks Orders, Per A Dietitian before you visit Starbucks the next time.

Subway's Spicy Italian

This sandwich combines two traditionally salty meats—pepperoni and salami—. A 6-inch sandwich with no cheese or sauce contains 480 calories and 1,520 mg of salt. A foot-long with mayo has 1180 calories and 3200 milligrams of salt. Instead, choose this: a 6-inch BLT on whole wheat with bacon, lettuce, and tomato. It contains fewer calories and less than half the salt (680 mg) (320).

Taco Bell Cinnabon Delights

The Cinnabon Delights at Taco Bell is one of the most well-liked menu items there, despite their odd appearance on a menu for a fast food restaurant with a Mexican theme. These cream cheese-frosted, sugar-coated cinnamon pastries are deep-fried.

Each Cinnabon Delight includes:

- 80 caloric
- A 4.5-gram fat
- Sodium 40 mg

You may eat more than two if you like cinnamon as much as I do. Cinnabon Delights have no nutritional benefit, unlike other menu items, including veggies like tomatoes, lettuce, and pickles. They'll make you grin for sure, but only sometimes eat them.

Taco Bell's Volcano Nachos

These molten cheese-covered nachos with spicy ground beef, pinto beans, and jalapenos have more salt (1,670 mg), fat (58 grams), and calories (970) than any other single item on the menu. Instead, choose this: Even though Nachos Supreme has chopped tomatoes, beans, nacho cheese, and spicy beef, it only has 430 calories, 23 grams of fat, and 690 milligrams of sodium.

Taco Bell -XXL Steak Burrito

Unsurprisingly, a fast food item with the word "XXL" in the name is a huge and unhealthy meal. Even less of a surprise when you learn that Taco Bell is responsible.

Despite having "low-fat sour cream" and including lettuce and tomatoes in some of their dishes, Taco Bell is not considered the healthiest restaurant. Due to the meat, cheese, rice, tortilla, and other hefty components in this Taco Bell burrito, there are around 1000 calories. Try their fresco-style burritos if you want Taco Bell but want something healthier.

The 2-piece Whitefish Fillet Combo from Long John Silver's

Long John Silver's menu star is cod, breaded in a salty batter. 1, and 80 mg of sodium are included in two pieces. The complete meal has 1,230 calories and 2,140 mg of sodium and comes with fries and a medium fountain drink. Instead, choose this: Order a la carte instead of skipping the combo. A nice trade-off would be two pieces of tilapia, a hush puppy, a corn cob better without butter or oil, and a small Diet Pepsi. It has 370 calories and just 760 mg of salt.

The Burger King Triple Whopper with Cheese

Burger King is most renowned for their flavorful, filling whoppers; when they are hungry, they will likely order the Triple Whopper. Three tender beef patties, tomatoes, cheese, lettuce, mayo, pickles, ketchup, and onions, are all included in the Triple Whopper with Cheese. Sandwiched between bread, these components have 1,216 calories. Additionally, this sandwich has a large amount of saturated fat—more than half the daily recommended amount. Consequently, even if you may want to feast like a king, it's crucial to understand what you're putting in your body.

· · ·

The Italian sausage marinara pasta dish from Domino's

Nutritional information per serving: There are 1,650mg of salt, 68g of carbs (3g of fiber, 13g of sugar), 27g of protein, and a total of 700 calories in this dish. The processed meats in this meal increase its salt load to 1650 mg. There are 36 grams of fat, 15 of which are saturated, and 0.5 are trans. The 700 calories, the fat, and the salt in this meal do not outweigh the 27 grams of protein it contains.

The Triple Bacon Jalapeno Cheeseburger from Wendy's

One thousand three hundred thirty calories, 95 g of fat (38 g saturated, 4.5 g trans), 2,150 mg of sodium, 43 g of carbohydrates (2 g fiber, 7 g sugar), and 76 g of protein make up the diet. "The Chipotle salad has more calories than this cheeseburger. Fries and beverages are not included in this. You will consume this 1,330-calorie bomb and feel hungry an hour later since it is loaded with inflammatory fats and deficient in fiber. There are healthier alternatives, and by selecting a burger with only one patty rather than three, you almost cut your calorie intake in half." — Castillo.

The Ultimate Breakfast Platter from Burger King

The Ultimate Breakfast Platter from Burger King contains every kind of carb and fat.

Most individuals choose biscuits, pancakes, and hash browns as breakfast foods if they want something hearty and delicious. You can order all three on this plate, eggs, and sausage, so you are not forced to decide. It is a full supper. However, it's also packed with more calories than you'll need in the morning unless you plan a long workout for that day.

. . .

Triple Flame-Broiled Whopper Sandwich from Burger King with Cheese

Nutrition: It has 82g of fat, 32g of saturated fat, zero grams of trans fat, 50g of carbohydrates, 2g of fiber, and 11g of sugar. It also has 72 grams of protein, 1,473 milligrams of sodium, 32g of saturated fat, and 82g of total fat. It contains 82 grams of fat, 32 of which are saturated (the recommended daily limit for saturated fat is 10 grams), and 4.5 grams of trans fat, which we want to avoid (they lower HDL and increase LDL). More than half of the daily recommended amount of salt is included in the sandwich at 1470 mg. The bread has no fiber and just simple carbohydrates.

Triple Whopper with Cheese from Burger King

Nutrition: A single serving contains 75g and 1,120mg of sodium, 4g of trans fat, 28g of saturated fat, 2g of dietary fiber, 49g of carbs, and 67g of protein. "The Dietary Guidelines for Americans recommend limiting your consumption of saturated fats to fewer than 10% of your total calories to lower your risk of getting heart disease. This sandwich alone has 126% of the recommended amount of saturated fat and 49% of the recommended amount of sodium based on a 2,000-calorie diet. These two figures should persuade you to remain far, far away." — Jonathan Valdez, R.D.N., proprietor of Genki Nutrition and a representative for the New York State Academy of Nutrition and Dietetics. If you want to protect your heart, this burger should be swapped out for foods that can help lower your risk of heart disease.

. . .

Turkey and Swiss sandwich from Starbucks

This sandwich has 390 calories and some crunchy leaf lettuce poking through. However, a brief inspection of the ingredients finds salt (1,140 mg of sodium) in the wheat bread, Swiss cheese, and turkey breast. Instead, choose this: Basil pesto on a roasted tomato and mozzarella panini (630 mg of sodium). You'll eat 510 mg less salt for the same amount of calories.

Wendy's Baconator

Given its reputation for burgers and icy beverages, it is no surprise that Wendy's dish enters this list.Due to its fresh 1/2 pound beef patties, Applewood-smoked bacon, and mouthwatering melted cheese, Wendy's Baconator is one of the fast-food restaurant's top-rated dishes. The ultimate burger for meat lovers! However, this is not the ideal option; if you're attempting, there are better options than to l. The Baconator has 1,010 calories, 67 grams of fat, and 38 grams of carbohydrates. Additionally, it contains a substantial amount of salt and sugar, two addictive elements.

Wendy's Baja Salad

Salt is provided by the toppings of this salad with a Southwest flavor profile, which includes chili, pico de gallo, guacamole, cheese, tortilla strips, and Creamy Red Jalapeno Dressing. The harm? Around 720 calories and 1,975 mg of salt. The dressing package has 100 calories and 270 mg of salt by itself. Instead, choose this: A tiny chili and a side salad from the garden. With about half the salt (910 mg) and two-thirds of the chili calories, you'll get the crunch you want in addition to the meaty richness of the dish (235).

. . .

Wendy's Pretzel Bacon Pub Triple

This meal has 1,520 calories, 106 grams of fat (45 grams of saturated fat and 4 grams of trans fat), 1,910 milligrams of sodium, 53 grams of carbs (3 grams of fiber and 7 grams of sugar), and 89 grams of protein. "This burger has the highest calorie count on the menu at 1,520 calories, 106 grams of fat, and 1,910 mg of sodium. It is advised that 20–35% of the calories in our diet come from fat, which translates to 44–77 grams of fat per 2,000 calories consumed. With 390 calories, 24 grams of fat, and 660 milligrams of sodium, the Jr. Bacon Cheeseburger might be a better choice.

Which low-sodium fast food dishes are the best?

With these dietitian-recommended orders, you may still use the drive-through if you are on a low-sodium diet. Are you trying to reduce salt consumption, or are you on a low-sodium diet because of conditions like high blood pressure? A drive-thru is still an option, even if the fast-food counter isn't the most fantastic place to start and doesn't deserve a regular presence in your healthy eating rotation.

1/2 Seasonal Greens Salad and a 1/2 Napa Almond Chicken Salad Sandwich from Panera - 470 mg of sodium

Due to Panera Bread's "half items in combos" policy, Swanson Health's Lindsey Toth, MS, RD orders half a Napa Almond Chicken Salad Sandwich and half a seasonal greens salad with reduced-fat balsamic vinaigrette. In addition, she will drink half of a glass of reduced-fat balsamic vinaigrette with her salad. This combo provides 470mg of salt and 16g of protein, making it a satisfying meal. Almonds may be rich in vitamin E, which is good for the skin. Healthy carotenoids like lutein and zeaxanthin are present in this fast food salad, helping to shield the eyes from the blue light emitted by our gadgets and computer displays.

8-count Grilled Chicken Nuggets from Chick-fil-A - 440 mg (515 mg if paired with half a packet of honey mustard sauce).

With just 140 calories and 19% of your DV for salt, this menu provides 25 grams of protein. Mix 515 milligrams of sodium with their Fruit Cup (0 mg) and 75 milligrams of sodium in half a package of honey mustard sauce. "Chick-fil-grilled A's chicken nuggets are a rich source of lean protein while being much lower in sodium ((540mg less salt than the regular Chick-fil-A nuggets' (8ct) serving))," If I use the dipping sauce sparingly, I'd still feel happy and full while avoiding too much salt. A fruit cup with no additional salt may be added to the order to offer a range of nutrients and fiber.

Arby's Roast Beef Slider with Jalapenos (Without cheese) - 470 mg

"It might be difficult to order a reduced sodium fast food meal at Arby's since bread, cheese, seasoned chicken, and pork are all rich in sodium. Here's where size does matter, "warned Brissette. "I advise getting one of Arby's sliders and leaving the cheese off rather than a traditional sandwich or gyro. The Jalapeo Roast Beef Slider has 470 mg of salt without the cheese (which, if ordered with the Swiss, might reduce your salt intake by 200 mg.). For some lemon or vinegar to be squeezed on top, serve it with a side salad." You might also request their Dijon Honey Mustard Dressing, which has the lowest sodium content on the menu. You may also get their Dijon Honey Mustard Dressing, which has the lowest sodium content of all the salad dressings. However, since the whole packet contains 230 milligrams of sodium, try to use just half of it.

Baked potato from Wendy's (with sour cream)- 40 mg

"When I'm pressed for time and have no alternatives, my go-to item is a Wendy's plain baked potato with only 40 milligrams of salt. For an additional 15 milligrams of salt, you may add sour cream and chives, "says a nutritionist at St. Francis Hospital in New York, Karen Z. Berg, MS, RD, CDN. "It's a full dish, so you know exactly what you're receiving, which is why I enjoy it. It offers only 270 calories and, as an extra benefit, 1,560 milligrams of potassium." Remember to include these potassium-rich foods in your diet if you want additional strategies to reduce bloating and relax your muscles.

Chick-fil-Greek A's Yogurt Parfait with Granola - 100 mg

A Chick-fil-A Yogurt Parfait with Granola is a healthy option if you watch your sodium intake. According to Yule, "This item is a bit higher in sugars than a savory meal (23 grams per serving), but that is mostly because of the fruit and the dairy in this item." The parfait has thirteen grams of protein, fifteen percent of the daily value for calcium, riboflavin derived from dairy, and phytochemicals derived from fruit. Additionally, with a serving size of 140 milligrams

of sodium, this product satisfies the FDA's established defin-
ition of a low-sodium food.

Chicken & Fajita Veggie Burrito Bowl from Chipotle - 490 mg

The well-known Mexican restaurant company doesn't
need a salt bomb in every meal. "I choose a Burrito Bowl
with chicken and fajita veggies, then top it with lettuce and
sour cream," explains Toth when he has a taste for Chipotle.
In addition to having 35 grams of protein, which promotes
strong muscles and makes me feel filled longer, this combo
has 490 milligrams of salt, much less than other menu
items.

Crunchy Taco with Beef, "Fresco Style," from Taco Bell - 270 mg

One Crunchy Taco with Beef ordered "Fresco Style,"
which excludes the Cheddar Cheese (30 calories/40 mg
sodium) and replaces it with zero-calorie/zero-sodium tomatoes, has 140 calories, 6 grams of protein, and 3 grams of
fiber. Because it has a respectable amount of protein and
fiber, this taco may be a filling snack, according to
Montemayor. It also has less salt than other tacos. If you
need to reduce your sodium consumption, eating two beef
tacos will give you less sodium (540 milligrams) than one
Taco Bell Beef Burrito Supreme (1,110 milligrams), making
them a full option.

Dunkin' Multigrain Oatmeal - 250 mg

This DDSmart oatmeal, with dried fruit on top, is a full and generally healthy way to start the day. "A whopping 7 grams of fiber are included, so you can expect to feel satisfied all morning long," says Berg. It has 250 milligrams of sodium (because it's instant). Although it contains some sugar, it is far less than the Munchkins looking up at you from the counter. Get advice from a professional at any coffee shop on remaining skinny while drinking that coffee.

Five Guy's Little Hamburger - 380 mg

According to Montemayor, A Little Hamburger from Five Guys contains 380 mg salt, which is rather low (17% DV), but that accounts for the bread and one patty. To prevent going overboard, read up on the nutrition information of each topping before adding it. Adding toppings may drastically boost salt levels. Try mustard, tomatoes, grilled/chopped onions, jalapenos, green peppers, and lettuce, advises Montemayor, to maintain salt levels in a healthy range.

Greek Vanilla Yogurt and Blueberry Parfait from Au Bon Pain - 115 mg

Greek yogurt, here we come. According to the authors of 21-Day Body Reboot, "The Nutrition Twins," the Greek vanilla yogurt and blueberry parfait from Au Bon Pain is a delicious choice for breakfast or lunch due to its sugary creaminess and fulfilling 24 grams of protein and 5 grams of fiber. You may feel great about yourself eating this since it has just 340 calories and 6 grams of fat.

· · ·

Half-Size Fuji Apple Salad with Chicken from Panera - 300 mg

According to Summer Yule, MS, RDN, "[This low-sodium fast food order only includes] 300 mg of salt per dish. This salad is low in calories (285), high in fiber (3 g), and protein (15 g).

Protein Style Hamburger from In-N-Out - 370 mg

This option has 240 calories and 370 milligrams of salt; however is used instead of bread. While preserving most of the characteristics of a conventional burger, ordering your burger "protein-style" may dramatically lower its salt level, according to Montemayor. "A hamburger has 370 milligrams of sodium without the bun, compared to 650 milligrams with the bread—saving you 280 milligrams if you order protein-style." By forgoing the bread, you will save 150 calories and 18 grams of carbohydrates. And, sure, this advice pertains to the hamburger. The salt content of one slice of cheese increases to 720 mg.

Starbucks' PB&J Protein Box - 570 mg

"This grab-and-go lunch box appeals to me since it has a well-balanced assortment of nutritious meals with diverse tastes and textures to intrigue your palate. You can find rich protein-packed peanut butter, soft whole grain bread, a tart yogurt dip with calcium, cheese, and crisp fruits and vegetables in one 520 calorie box, "Maggie Moon, MS, RD, a Los Angeles-based dietitian and the author of The MIND Diet, offers her thoughts on this box order with 570 milligrams of sodium.

. . .

The PB&J Protein box has 20 grams of satisfying protein, 18 grams of the brain- and heart-healthy unsaturated fats, and 20% of your daily fiber requirements (five grams), which will keep you full for hours.

Steel-cut oatmeal from Panera with almonds, quinoa, and honey - 150 mg

Looking for a Panera breakfast option with reduced sodium? According to Chef Julie Harrington, RD, "[it] includes] only 150 milligrams of sodium, providing just 9% of the necessary amount of salt prescribed for the day," making it a wonderful choice. I like the addition of quinoa to steel-cut oats because it introduces ancient grains in novel ways while adding a nutty taste and texture. With the addition of protein- and fiber-rich quinoa and almonds, each serving of this dish clocks in at 320 calories with just 7 grams of sugar.

Subway's 6" Veggie Delite - 240 mg

You will find a few low-sodium options at Subway, but finding anything better than this Veggie Delight sandwich is challenging. One 6-inch Subway sandwich on their 9-Grain Wheat bread has 190 calories, 2 grams of total fat, 39g of carbohydrates, 5g of fiber, 6 grams of sugar, and 9 grams of protein. This amounts to 12 percent of the daily value of salt. According to Montemayor, this is one of the lowest sodium selections on the Subway menu for those with salt restrictions. According to Montemayor, Swiss cheese may increase the sandwich's protein content without making it too heavy on the high-sodium cold cuts. This addition increases the protein to 13 grams while the sodium stays at 310 milligrams, or 13% DV. The author continues that the sandwich's two servings of veggies, high vitamin A and C content, and an excellent source of iron are just a few of its many advantages. Pritikin Longevity Center's director of nutrition Kimberly Gomer, MS, RD, LDN, recommends serving your sandwich with "a great large apple or another piece of fruit you've brought from home." This way, you're not only eating well but also feeling satisfied.

The Fruit and Maple Oatmeal from McDonald's - 140 mg (260 mg with a side of scrambled eggs)

"Even when you believe you're choosing a better option, like a salad with chicken, it's incredibly challenging to consume a low sodium fast food order at McDonald's. Now that they provide breakfast all day, I'll order breakfast items whenever I go, "says 80 Twenty Nutrition President Christy Brissette, MS, RD. "I'll have the Fruit and Maple Oatmeal with 140 milligrams of salt, please (without the brown sugar). She continues, "I'll also buy a side order of two scrambled eggs, which include 120 milligrams of salt to get extra protein," bringing the sodium content of the whole meal to 260 milligrams.

The Protein Bistro Box from Starbucks - 540 mg

Want some vigor? Substitute the pastries with this low-sodium Eggs & Cheese Protein Box, which has 470 calories and 23 grams of protein. According to Nutritional specialists, this package of full, unprocessed meals contains a hard-boiled egg, natural nut butter, fruit, cheese, and a little raisin muffin for the nut butter. "The salt content of Starbucks' other boxes is far lower than that of typical fast food items, which often have 1,000 mg or more of sodium per serving. These choices include fresh fruit and vegetables in portion-controlled containers and better quality ingredients."

Vegan Pineapple Spinach Smoothie from Smoothie King - 170 mg

Consider this 360-calorie smoothie, 170 milligrams of salt, a light lunch, or a satisfying post-workout protein drink. "To help you acquire the necessary vegetables, the Vegan Pineapple Spinach mix contains organic spinach and carrots. Additionally, it provides more than 30% of your daily fiber needs and is a rich source of protein, "explains nutrition and weight reduction specialist Samantha Cassetty, MS, RD. "You could always personalize your mix with additional protein (and more vegetables!) for those that need a bit more." Include the national chain Smoothie King on your permitted food list since many of its mixes don't include artificial colors, flavors, or preservatives and are very low in sugar.

Veggie Lovers Small Thin 'N Crispy Slice from Pizza Hut - 270 mg

You know all too well that desiring a piece of pie may result in a few days later becoming friends with a whole pie on your sofa. Instead, give in to your need and order a piece of Pizza Hut's veggie-loaded pizza. Most people believe that eating pizza would break their calorie and salt budgets. Still, with just 100 calories per slice, you also receive an added health benefit from the vegetables' antioxidants and other nutrients, "The Nutrition Twins assert. Additionally, a slice may be enjoyed without fearing that the 3.5 grams or the 1.5 grams of saturated fat would harm your health or weight.

Final Thoughts

Consider your decision before ingesting them since these are the unhealthiest fast food options.

These meaty, cheesy, and carb-heavy meals are popular because of their high fat, sugar, and salt quantities. The flavor and joy of biting into these juicy, crunchy, and savory foods are adored by consumers.

While treating yourself once in a while is OK, regularly consuming these foods might result in weight gain, health issues, and a generally unhealthier lifestyle.

Check the nutritional facts the next time you're at a fast-food restaurant to decide if you want to eat one of these things or something healthier.

The key feature of this chapter

- Limit your intake to one slice and finish your meal with low-sodium items, such as a leafy green salad with a low-sodium dressing.
- Instead, choose fresh foods or canned goods with less salt.
- You learned of the unhealthiest fast-food products to avoid in this chapter
- The Dietary Guidelines for Americans recommend limiting your consumption of saturated fats to fewer than 10% of your total calories to lower your risk of getting heart disease.

Dear Reader,

As independent authors, it's often difficult to gather reviews compared with much bigger publishers.

Therefore, please leave a review on the platform where you bought this book.

KINDLE:

[LEAVE A REVIEW HERE < click here >](#)

Many thanks,

Author Team

CONCLUSION

In conclusion, low-sodium eating can be an incredible and delicious journey toward improved health and wellness. Protecting your heart and lowering your risk of high blood pressure and other health concerns may be as simple as controlling the amount of salt you eat daily. We hope this book has provided you with the information and tools to make low-sodium eating a part of your lifestyle. No matter how much you know about cooking, the recipes and tips in this book will help you create tasty, healthy, and low-sodium meals. Reducing sodium intake takes time and effort, but your health and well-being benefits are worth it. Be patient, persistent, and, most importantly, enjoy the process. Low-sodium eating is full of flavor, variety, and endless possibilities.

Also, it's important to remember that low-sodium eating isn't just about cutting out salt and avoiding high-sodium foods. It's also about eating a healthy, balanced diet. Fruits, vegetables, whole grains, and lean meats are all examples of entire foods that might provide the nourishment your body needs to thrive. Additionally, it's a good idea to use your imagination and experiment with various spices and seasonings to give the flavor of your meal. Try new herbs and spices, such as basil, rosemary, thyme, or garlic, and discover how they can transform the taste of your dishes.

Finally, feel free to change your diet as needed. That which helps one individual may not help another is acceptable. To make low-sodium eating a sustainable and enjoyable part of your life, you must figure out what works best for you. So, continue to educate yourself on low-sodium eating, experiment with new recipes, and, most importantly, listen to your body. Your health is worth the effort, and low-sodium eating can be a delicious and fulfilling journey with the right tools and information.

We appreciate your participation in this adventure. We wish you the best as you try to eat less salt, and we hope you keep making healthy choices so you can live a happy and healthy life.

Made in United States
Troutdale, OR
10/08/2023

13499001R00141